T0004090

The Back Page

The
Back Page

A Life in Sport

By Steve Millar

Fifty Years
of Headlining
with Sporting
Kings

First published by Pitch Publishing, 2022

Pitch Publishing
9 Donnington Park,
85 Birdham Road,
Chichester,
West Sussex,
PO20 7AJ
www.pitchpublishing.co.uk
info@pitchpublishing.co.uk

© 2022, Steve Millar

Every effort has been made to trace the copyright.
Any oversight will be rectified in future editions at the
earliest opportunity by the publisher.

All rights reserved. No part of this book may be reproduced,
sold or utilised in any form or transmitted in any form or by
any means, electronic or mechanical, including photocopying,
recording or by any information storage and retrieval system,
without prior permission in writing from the Publisher.

A CIP catalogue record is available for this book
from the British Library.

ISBN 978 1 80150 207 8

Typesetting and origination by Pitch Publishing
Printed and bound in India by Replika Press Pvt. Ltd.

CONTENTS

CHAPTER 1

THE CALL came out of the Algarve blue as I stretched my creaky bones to shuffle off the sunbed to answer my mobile in the kitchen of our Coelha beach holiday apartment. It was the *Daily Star* Sunday office back in Bamber Bridge near Preston. The sports editor, a fresh-faced rookie called Michael Ham, had bad news to darken the holiday mood.

'Steve, I've had a call from the management and they are looking at sports desk cuts. I'm afraid your job is at risk,' he coolly and calmly reported in a detached manner.

That was back in September 2018. And eight months later, after a reprieve while the bosses deliberated and reluctantly agreed to a modest pay-off, the axe fell brutally to sever 50 years in journalism, man and boy.

I admit I felt isolated, especially when the good luck phone calls stopped. I wasn't ready for retirement and felt I'd been elbowed into obscurity. The job I loved was no longer. At 67 I felt I had another 12 months to professionally cover the role I was born to fulfil. Anyway, I wanted to leave on my terms and not suffer the knee-jerk reaction of some suit in London.

Despair with a capital 'D' saturated my body, my scrambled mind unable to face the reality of waking up every morning without a phone call to the office or a press conference to attend. But in the following months of feeling that I'd been scrubbed from the journalistic history books as the forgotten man, I remembered wise words from the legend that is Sir Alex Ferguson.

Fergie himself was nearing the day he'd turn off the infamous hairdryer for the final time and pulled me to one side after a Manchester United press conference at the club's Carrington training ground.

'Whatever you do Steve, when the big day comes and you retire, always keep your brain on the go. When that switches off, so does your ticker,' the great man informed me with a serious look in the eye.

So, here I am, keeping the brain cells active with a nostalgic, and I hope humorous, look back through the half-century of years to when my career started with my very first job in journalism.

I was just a teenager living in a Manchester overspill estate called Partington with dad Stan, mum Pat and sister Anne. College was over and I'd somehow scraped through from two years at Timperley with five GCE 'O' levels to my name.

And then came the lightbulb moment with a quick look through the Partington edition of the *Stretford and Urmston Journal* back in the summer of 1968. There on the back page was an advert looking for a trainee reporter with the proviso that the applicant must have five 'O' levels, including English language.

Bingo. That's me, I thought, and I applied for the big job, being told for certain that I was the only one in Partington with those qualifications. Sure enough, the editor, Maurice Brown, was happy to take me on, so the incredible journey began from Urmston to Manchester to the far-flung lands of Singapore, Japan, South Africa and infinity and beyond.

It was a great four-year training period under the guidance of editor and *Sunday Mirror* Saturday casual Maurice, plus fellow reporters Trevor Coombes, Angela Kelly and little Bob Bayliss. I learned everything about the job, from calling in every morning at the Urmston police station to scribble down the previous night's incidents to covering courts, inquests, road traffic accidents and golden weddings – I couldn't believe anyone could be hitched for 50 years. I know now.

The *Journal* offices were based in the centre of Urmston, a location right up my dad Stan's street, so to speak. He worked around the corner as a postman at the local delivery office and I lost count of the number of times reception would call upstairs to tell me, 'Steve, your dad's here to see you.'

The words never altered. 'Son, can you spare a couple of quid? I've got a cert running in the 2.30 at Doncaster.' I always coughed up but the bookies never did.

How could I say no, though, to the Belfast man who brought me into this world after marrying my mum Pat at RAF Changi, Singapore, where they were both stationed? I arrived on this earth on 15 July 1951, just nine months after they tied the knot, sparking endless family jokes that

I was born with a broken hand – trying to hold on until after the wedding.

Stan did well to get Pat's hand in marriage after she'd first dated future stage and TV legend Bruce Forsyth, who worked with her in the RAF station's signals room. Obviously my dad played his cards right.

I'm told my first few months on the planet were shared with chameleons falling from the ceiling on to my cot net, and a pet monkey bought by my dad, who wasn't the happiest at saying goodbye to Singapore to return to England. Reluctantly, he boarded the ship to sail him home, supposedly alongside mum and me. But that was the last we saw of him, Mum said, for the whole six-week voyage. Stan spent every day with aircrew, eating and drinking in the mess before bedding down every night in his bunk absent of wife and child.

He was certainly a character, my old man, happy to please my Roman Catholic mum by converting to her faith to marry and renouncing his strict Protestant background after being brought up in Argyll Street, Belfast, just off the Shankill Road. Stan didn't have the courage to tell his family of Orangemen on his return home that he'd taken Catholic vows and Holy Communion, such was the hatred of the religious enemy. His silence lasted seven years before his dad William – a riveter on the Titanic – and the Orange Lodge brothers were informed and, amazingly, accepted his switch to the enemy camp without rancour.

During that long period of sectarian silence, we'd visit the Irish folks on a regular basis and would be strictly sworn to secrecy. I was innocent of the hatred of

Catholics in the Millar family's Protestant stronghold and wonder now what they would have thought of me, later educated by nuns at a convent near RAF Lindholme, Doncaster.

Funny now to think back to the days when I'd sit on the step of their terraced house in Argyll Street drawing pictures of priests at altars with me as an altar boy. Christ, my dad would go mad and rip up the evidence before you could say Holy Sh**. I still smile about how I was probably only the one Catholic to walk in Orange Day parades through the streets of Belfast with my unsuspecting uncles. Not a bad claim to fame.

Yes, I was heavily into religion in those early, formative years of mine. I became an altar boy at RAF Lindholme's Roman Catholic church and was happy to serve the local priest at every Mass. In fact, I got so wrapped up in the religious world that I wondered whether one day I'd become a priest. The nuns had always told me that if I ever got the calling from above I should answer 'yes'.

Every day I dreaded getting that heavenly thumbs-up. I didn't want to be a priest and I was scared God would summon me to the priesthood. The only thing I liked about living the Catholic altar life was having a sly slug of the altar wine in the vestry after every service.

I think that's where my love of drink started – as a seven-year-old. That and getting an egg cup filled with Guinness from my grandma Kitty every Sunday when we came back from Mass at Withington Hospital.

She was a character. Kitty was born the illegitimate daughter of her mum, a maid in then affluent Moss Side in

Manchester who never saw husband Jack for all five years of the Second World War.

Jack the Lad joined up with the Royal Marines in 1939, was posted to Portsmouth, and for some reason never left these shores, getting Marine pals to send postcards to Kitty from their battlefields in France. I was always told as well that Jack had a secret family in Portsmouth, with kids from the 'marriage' who we obviously never met.

Kitty was a wonderful, wonderful lady. Imagine now being born in 1900 before planes and automobiles and living through two world wars, seeking bomb shelters in the garden at the height of the Manchester bombings.

I promised I'd write a book like this about her amazing life but never fulfilled it. I really regret not penning her life story for my kids and grandchildren to read. A truly remarkable life and lady. I can still see Kitty now in a powder-blue coat and matching hat held on by a massive hat pin. And I can still recall leaving her one day in my Ford Capri while I shopped in her home town of Chorlton-cum-Hardy. On my return an hour later I discovered Kitty almost unconscious on the back seat as she sweltered in her coat and hat on one of the hottest days of the year. Imagine that, killing your own granny. Sorry Kitty.

Kitty, I must add, lived the last 40 or so years of her life with a glass eye, a scary sight for a kid growing up. And I was still haunted when I, wife Syl and sister Anne went to Wharton Avenue in Chorlton to clear out her belongings after her death.

I wondered all day whether we'd come across her spare eye, and sure enough, when I cleared the last room of the house, her downstairs bathroom, I found a tiny wicker box.

Nervously lifting the lid, there it was. The blue eye. Christ, I swept the box into a bin bag and hurriedly stuffed it into the boot of my Capri. Then, to my horror, the bag toppled and out popped the box containing the eye, which rolled all the way down Wharton Avenue, where it stayed. I couldn't have asked neighbours whether they had seen a rolling eye, could I?

Back to normality. My early life was totally entrusted to the armed forces, remembering as a toddler living on a base in Cirencester before Dad's posting to RAF Oldenburg in Germany, where my sister Anne was born.

I still remember the first time I saw baby Anne in hospital along with my dad. My mum cradled Anne in her arms and handed me a present from my new sister. A red London bus and a letter saying how proud she was to have me as a big brother. I couldn't believe it. If she couldn't even walk, how could she get to the shops to buy the bus, let alone write me a letter? But then again, she always was the clever one of the two siblings.

I went to the local school, and although I can't remember a word now, I did speak a little German and can still recall singing a local song that I think was on the lines of 'Fire, fire henschun'. Or something similar lost in the translation.

Looking back now, mine was a joyous life, which could have been cruelly cut short at just five or six years old when Mum and Dad took me and my baby sister on a trip to Winterberg, a winter resort in western Germany. It's famous for its ski slopes and massive ski jump. Certainly an impressive place for a wide-eyed kid who wanted to take a better look at this impressive resort.

So Dad took me up to the top of a watchtower to gaze at the exciting panorama, but a high wall on the viewing floor prevented a proper look for this inquisitive child. So I took a run and jump and reached out for the top of the wall, only to horrifically misjudge the height and start to slide head-first, 100 feet to the ground. Thankfully, Dad was alert and grabbed my legs to basically save my life. Thanks super Stan.

We returned to England after three years at Oldenburg and had temporary transit accommodation in Blackpool, where this German-speaking kid helped out on the Pleasure Beach. The Love Boat ride to be precise, dragging in the craft after loved-up couples had departed for dry land.

Stan's next move was to RAF Lindholme, where Anne and I were taught by those nuns at the convent in Stainforth near Doncaster. I was into my writing even then as a confident nine-year-old but, suddenly, for no reason, I developed a serious stutter – a curse quickly picked up on by the cruel teaching nuns.

The morning register became a nightmare, with the daunting prospect of having to answer to the question: 'Stephen Millar?' To which I had to reply: 'Present Sister De Lestenac.' Well, you can imagine how difficult those explosive words were to a boy with a stammer. So I hoped to get round it by stuttering, 'Present ster ...' That clearly wasn't good enough, and although she knew about my horrible speech impediment, Sister De Lestenac made me stand in front of class for ten minutes, stuttering away to my complete embarrassment amid the class laughter.

As I grew, the stutter began to ease and my confidence returned with a move to senior school at St Peter's Comprehensive in Doncaster. I was in the grammar stream and my love for writing developed even more, with essays marked highly by the teachers.

My football skills were praised, too, although I had trouble getting into the first XI at my favoured position, right-back. I still don't know why, other than the automatic choice was some little snotty kid called Kevin Keegan. I reminded Kevin about breaking my footballing heart generations later at a charity dinner at Blackpool FC, before Christmas 2021.

Okay, fair enough, he may have played 230 times for Liverpool, scoring 68 goals and winning 63 England caps. Oh, and he managed our country, Newcastle, Fulham and Manchester City. But did he really think that he was a better footballer than me and deserved to play in the St Peter's XI ahead of Steve Millar? Kev, on tiptoes, looked me in the eyes and smiled that knowing smile. Sorry mate, that's where we begin to differ. I too was a great player – and a lot taller.

He played another part in my life later, when in 1980 he was playing for Hamburg. My colleague Vince Wilson ghosted Kev's column in our *Sunday Mirror* newspaper, for which he was paid an incredible £30,000 a year. Vince told me that Kev had revealed he was signing for Southampton and the sensational move would be announced on 11 February 1980 by Saints boss Lawrie McMenemy.

What a great scoop for us then on a sensational Sunday. At least that's what Vince, sports editor Peter Shaw and I thought, as I started to design the back page and inside spread.

That was until Lawrie told Vince that we couldn't print a word of our would-be world exclusive because Southampton wanted to surprise the footballing world on 11 February, a Monday. Thanks Lawrie – and thanks again Kev that we couldn't break the big one 24 hours before he was unveiled as Southampton's new signing in a plush city centre hotel. We should have published and been damned.

Anyway, back to Doncaster and RAF Lindholme, which was a great place for a kid to grow up, especially in the summer holidays when officers would agree to decommission a veteran bomber, mainly Wellingtons. The twin-engine long-range Wellington would be towed to the far side of the airfield and us RAF kids would be invited to play on this Second World War veteran of the skies.

Nothing was off-limit. We'd buckle up in the cockpit or take a seat in the rear bomber glass dome with the guns still in position. Or we could climb out on to the wings and release the rubber dinghy to ride on it to the runway below. Helmets and goggles were stored in the cockpit, so the fun, as you can see, multiplied for us excited kids.

Imagine that scene today, with health and safety fanatics ruling the world. No way would we have been allowed to clamber all over a world war flying machine, pretending to shoot the Luftwaffe out of the Doncaster skies.

Back down to earth again, and my next school was at Casterton near Oakham in Rutland, when Dad, now a corporal, was posted to RAF Cottesmore. My sense of humour and the desire to be the class favourite showed no bounds.

I thought one day that it would be funny to lift the lid on the geography teacher's desk and take and hide his white, size 12 plimsoll he used to smack class-mates across the bum for indiscretions. I placed it in the desk of a kid I didn't like, and when Sir looked for his punishment pump, he demanded to know where it was. The nerd pointed to me and the teacher immediately summoned misbehaving Millar out of class. The school bell was rung and every girl and boy pupil assembled around the playground, where I was frogmarched into the middle, with the geography teacher pulling down my shorts and underpants for a bare-arsed flogging. Imagine that happening now. The teacher would be jailed.

Anyway, the bum deal made me think. Obviously. Later school years saw me develop into a more sensible student with prefect jobs at St Pius the Tenth in Rusholme, Manchester, after Stan left the RAF because he didn't want to take the family to Aden at the start of the Arab uprising in the early 60s.

It was an arduous journey to St Pius the Tenth, taking two buses from Partington. But I was happy at the school, where one of my class-mates was Moors murder victim Keith Bennett. What a bloody horror story.

My final school was Blessed Thomas Halford in Altrincham, Cheshire, where I became head boy – carefully distancing myself from one of my good pals, Steve Derbyshire. Derby had somehow decided that the final terms of school weren't for him, so he missed two of them by playing truant. Every morning his mum would pack his school bag, hand him his blazer and wave him off at the door. Steve would hide around the corner, wait until she'd left for work, then nip back home and spend the day in the shed.

Unlike Steve, I loved school. Loved the sports fields and stage where I starred as a Chinese officer in 'A Letter from the General.'

And then it was off to further education when I enrolled at Timperley College just down the road to study in a two-year commercial course, which taught me the typing and shorthand skills later used successfully in journalism.

I often think back to those treasured school days – apart from the playground beating – and cast my mind back to those Belfast trips of keeping tight-lipped about Dad's Catholic vows. Stan would often laugh about the deception, but although a convert to the Catholic faith, the Ulsterman in him was deeply engraved. Stan, as I said, loved his horses, football – and drinking, of course. When I was 16, he walked me from our Partington home to the nearest boozer, the Saracen's Head at Warburton, and asked me what I wanted to drink. I asked for a coke but he thrust a pint of bitter in my hand and said, 'If you're going to drink, I want you to sup beer in front of me and not behind my back.'

Great advice. He had that in abundance. Stan always told me to shake another man's hand with the firmest of grips and to look him in the eye. He also coated me one day for disappearing into the toilet when it was my round to buy him and his brothers pints in a Shankill pub.

'What are you bloody doing?' he barked out in the urinal when he caught me counting out my money in my hand. 'If you can't afford to buy your round then don't bloody come into the pub.'

I learned so much from Dad, who was taken away way too early at the age of 44 on 16 December 1970, just as we were getting to know each other as men with regular pint-supping nights.

I received the dreaded call from the police when I was in the *Stretford and Urmston Journal* office. They informed me that he'd been rushed into Park Hospital, Davyhulme, after collapsing in the street. I drove like a madman to the critical care unit, explaining over and over again that he was only 44. A fit man who walked miles every day as a postman. He'd done 30 press-ups the other night, I told the medics.

But Dad didn't stand a chance and never regained consciousness from a brain clot, passing away the following morning with me, Mum and Uncle Peter by his bedside. Our broken hearts never ever mended.

I had to identify my own dad in the morgue. And I can still picture the scene as the white sheet was peeled back to reveal my dear dad's handsome face. God, that was hard to take. My dad. Dead. Park Hospital filled me with dread from that moronic morning – although later events in its wards did finally return a smile to my face.

I feel uncomfortable recalling one mad moment but, hey, here goes. I was quite friendly with Bernard from the mortuary after meeting him while reporting inquests. He had a wicked sense of humour just like me, and when my mum was admitted for heart checks, I devised a plan. I told Bernard which ward Pat was on and, following my instructions, he got his tape measure out and sized her up from the top of her head to the bottom of her feet. Mum told me later (after a huge telling-off on my part) that she asked Bernard what the bloody hell he was doing.

'Just measuring you up for the coffin if anything goes wrong,' he told a startled, horrified Mrs Millar, who clearly didn't see the funny side when he said it was Stephen's little joke. Oops!

Mind you, the smile was back on Mum's face many years later when in the same hospital my wife Sylvia gave birth first to Nicola on 30 December 1975, followed by Anthony on 11 January 1978, to make our life complete.

But before then, my newspaper adventure was really developing at the *Journal*, with mentor Maurice polishing the rough diamond in his charge.

I made good contacts around the Stretford and Urmston area. None more so than the young CID lads at the nearby nick, who became good drinking buddies. I'll never forget one night before Christmas when they invited me to their police party at The Wishing Well Club in Swinton, where legendary comedian Bernard Manning was top of the bill. After a boozy night we got a taxi back to Urmston where I'd parked my sky-blue Ford Escort with a dent on the bonnet in the station's car park behind the cop shop.

Well, the madness continued inside with the detectives letting off fire alarms in Urmston shopping centre in the early hours. We drank whisky, beer, anything alcoholic in fact, and at 3am I felt I'd had enough and asked them to call me a taxi.

'Taxi?' one said. 'You've got your car outside. Drive that.' I just laughed and pointed out my distressed, alcohol-blasted body.

'Are you serious?' I answered. 'How can I drive home when I'm so pi**ed – I'll get done by the cops.'

Within minutes they had solved my predicament as they called for two Panda cars with flashing lights to escort me and my car back to Partington, with one at the front, the other at the rear. The journey through one eye was a success.

Yes, there were many, many lighter moments working on my first newspaper – and darker times, too.

I'll never forget 14 April 1970, when I caught the bus to Urmston only to be turned back at the office by editor Maurice. News had just come through of a major incident on the Manchester Ship Canal near my Partington home. Workers who had boarded a boat at Bobs Ferry – the ship canal crossing to Cadishead – had been engulfed by 60-foot flames in what became known as the Partington Ferry Disaster.

Seemingly, a tanker being loaded at the Shell Chemicals Partington basin had leaked fuel and chemicals flooded into the canal. The tide of death had floated down to the ferry crossing. It's understood that one passenger discarded a cigarette into the water and the explosion could be heard ten miles away, with nearby Lock Lane in Partington being evacuated.

I could only venture as far as the police cordon at the top of the path leading down to the ferry decking and I waited all day for news of any victims. Tragically, there were six fatalities, including my mate from Partington, Brian Hillier. What a shock. My footballing pal burned to death and his body was recovered a week later. That was one difficult, tearful story to write.

Four years later another close Partington pal, Michael Waugh, was killed along with ten other soldiers when the IRA blew up a coach carrying army heroes back to camp in Catterick. The vehicle had only just left Manchester and was travelling to the top of the M62 in Yorkshire when the bomb on board detonated. Michael, God bless him, was just 22.

CHAPTER 2

IT WAS time for my next step on the journey to hopefully the top in journalism as my mind turned seriously to a future in sport writing.

I'd meddled with football on the *Journal*, writing up match reports of my team, Partington Village, and subbing them into the back page of the local edition. I couldn't resist, but because I was the reporter somehow I always got the Star Player award. Funny that.

But I had my serious hat on when I heard the *Evening Post and Chronicle* were looking for a news reporter at their base in Wigan back in 1972. I knew there would be a chance down the road to do a sports subbing shift on my Saturday day off.

I held my breath. I desperately wanted to move onwards and upwards, and in the end the switch up the M6 to Wigan paid off in a massive way. The work was varied, with daily visits to the magistrates' court reporting on various cases and a wide variety of news stories to crack.

I remember one blockbuster that gave me a glimpse into the lucrative world of national newspapers. It was soon after I started working at the *Evening Post and Chronicle* that news came in of a tanker spillage in a crash on the M6 at Billinge. Deadly acid had spurted from the wreck and washed down the three lanes of the motorway. Drivers remained marooned in their cars until the arrival of fire crews and ambulances. One particular paramedic had splashed through the acid to carry victims to the safety of the hard shoulder embankment and I got front-page projection with his brave account of his heroics.

A week later he phoned me in the office to tell the harrowing story of the aftermath. Seemingly, he'd put in a claim to the ambulance service for his boots, which had badly perished running through the acid. But, amazingly, his claim had been rejected because the damage wasn't, the pen-pushers said, fair wear and tear. Christ, are you kidding? How the hell could you snub such a heroic paramedic?

However, that produced a great, compelling follow-up, and a call to the *Daily Mail* news desk in Manchester. The news editor couldn't hide his delight and put me straight on to the copy takers. Sure enough, the next day the acid splash story was literally splashed over the news pages and I was later sent a cheque for £50, which paid for a holiday to Abersoch. I couldn't believe the amount of money the *Daily Mail* paid, although I was to find out just how much in wages when I joined their ranks some time later.

But back to the *Evening Post and Chronicle* and an unexpected call one day to see whether I'd be interested in covering Wigan Athletic in the Northern Premier League.

I didn't hesitate to burst out with a 'yes, yes, yes' reply and the job was mine.

I loved every minute of every match, with a team filled with huge characters in the non-league game. Scousers John Rogers and Johnny King were not only good players but great fun to be around. And around I was.

Wigan in those days, before finally being elected to the Football League, were the mega-bucks Manchester United of the non-league scene. Every away match was done in style, with a Friday night meet-up in the Brocket Arms pub followed by a luxury coach journey to the best hotels on our travels. I was treated as one of the squad, the local Wigan Athletic reporter, sharing hotel rooms and after-match meals. One of the boys.

It was a memorable one-and-only season, which culminated in the Latics reaching the FA Trophy Final in 1973, where they were to play at Wembley for the first time. Photographer Frank Burrows and I climbed aboard the team coach on that Thursday morning in April and, after a meal on the way, booked into our plush Hemel Hempstead hotel.

At night, Frank and I went out for a meal and a few drinks, and stayed on the ale far too long. We were now worse for wear and desperate to get back for a good night's kip. So it seemed a good idea at the time to try to thumb a lift at a roundabout outside the pub. I remember through the haze of a snakebite or two (cider and lager) a posh limo approaching our direction, so we cheekily stuck out a thumb. The driver didn't stop, much to our disgust. So we stepped out into the road, waving furious V-signs. The sound of braking would have woken the Hemel Hempstead dead, and within a few seconds the limo was reversing at high speed towards two startled journalists.

I looked at Frank and he looked at me as the two occupants flung the doors open to run towards us, waving fists and screaming obscenities. It turned out they were two of the famous pop group the Barron Knights returning from a gig. Pete Langford and Butch Baker wanted to fight and jostled into me and Frank with fists, threatening to spoil our looks for the big day at Wembley.

After threats and cold stares we turned and, naturally, fled, calling them a shite band anyway who couldn't lace the Beatles' boots. We were right there. Thank God we managed to flag down a taxi and laugh about our near slaying by the Knights.

We were still giggling over breakfast but got our sensible heads on to join the squad on a pre-final visit to Wembley. Just walking out on to the pitch was a privilege. Touching the hallowed turf where seven years earlier Bobby Moore and those other 1966 England legends had lifted the World Cup.

We couldn't resist walking up those famous steps to the Royal Box and pretending to hold aloft a trophy ourselves on the very spot where Bobby had received the coveted Jules Rimet trophy. And then the fun began in earnest with a look behind the scenes at the Queen's private quarters. I can still remember the feeling of sitting on her majesty's 'throne' and wondering whether I'd committed a crime parking my own bum on a toilet seat reserved for the Queen.

Needless to say, it was a real bummer of a match the following day, with Scarborough beating Les Rigby-led Wigan 2-1 in front of a bumper 23,000 crowd. It was a real downer after 48 hours of never-to-be-forgotten fun before the big match. But we weren't down for long with an after-match banquet at the Esso Motor Hotel at Wembley to be enjoyed, alongside my girlfriend and future wife Sylvia who had arrived that morning with the players' wives and girlfriends. Strangely, even though the Latics lads had lost at Wembley, there was nothing morose about that Saturday night, with food and drink flowing in great quantities.

Syl had thoroughly enjoyed being treated as a 'player's wife' on the journey down to London in their own drink-laden luxury coach and we danced until the small hours in those heady days when my knees didn't ache.

Back then, trips to the dance floor were plentiful. We first met in the Blue Rooms in Sale, where on my way to buy a pint of Watney's Red Barrel, I'd first spotted the teenage Syl out dancing with her mates. I can still feel the flutter of when I stared at her face but, me being me, I never committed in those early years and basically treated her badly until I came to my senses after my dad died.

Syl later worked at the *Evening Post and Chronicle* as a Saturday copy taker, and 12 months after the Wembley knees-up we were celebrating our wedding on 25 May 1974.

That was also the year my life would take another turn, with a tip-off that the *Daily Mail* in Manchester were looking for a news sub-editor. I really wanted a sports desk job but joining a national newspaper was a real step in the right direction, so I got on board.

CHAPTER 3

LIFE WAS good. Sylvia and I married at St John's Church in Brooklands, Sale, where her three sisters Lynda, Ann and Pam had all tied the knot with Geoff, Paul and John, respectively. Syl's dad Harry proudly walked her down the aisle to a nervous future husband standing at the front of the church alongside my best man Phil Gorton, brother of our Partington Village team-mate Chris. My sister Anne was maid of honour, followed by our bridesmaids, nieces Joanne and Cathy.

The service was nerve-wracking but beautiful at the same time, with my thoughts flashing to how even more perfect the day would have been if my dad and Syl's mum Lily had been alive and beaming with delight in the congregation.

I'd wanted to later take the wedding party to my own church in Partington, Our Lady of Lourdes, for a blessing because of my Catholic upbringing but the pompous priest wouldn't entertain it. He told me directly, 'If you walk down the aisle of a Protestant church you won't be married in the eyes of God.'

Well that was that then. So it was over to Brooklands and a walk down the aisle of a Protestant church with a two-finger vision to my priest firmly set in my mind.

At night, we enjoyed a fabulous reception at Painter's Studio in Urmston – just around the corner from my cop shop pals. The next day came the honeymoon in the Lake District, where we'd booked seven nights at the Calder Bridge Hotel near Seascale, with its tiny windows covered in ivy. We went out for a meal and returned to the hotel bar, which resembled a scene from an Alfred Hitchcock thriller. There were the millionaire couple, the attractive blonde on her own and a guy who looked like a colonel – all staring at the newlyweds.

We couldn't wait to say our goodnight and entered our mini-suite, romantically named 'The Nockin Room'. Bizarrely, there was no lock or key. Strange that, I thought. Anyway, clothes off, shower and off to bed, only for Sylvia to end my peaceful slumber in the early hours with an elbow dig in the ribs.

'Steve, wake up, wake up,' my new wife whispered. 'Look at that in the corner. It's a monk with a hood hiding his face. Oh my god, he's walking towards us. Christ, Steve, look.'

I didn't. Bravely, I hid under the sheets until whatever it was vanished. As you can imagine, sleep didn't come easily after that and morning couldn't come quickly enough.

Breakfast was consumed in a rush followed by a visit to reception to look at the brochures on the history of the hotel. We both stared at each other goggle-eyed after reading that the building was originally a … monastery! That seven-night stay became just one and we packed our bags for a quick getaway to the sanctuary of The Grey Walls Hotel in Windermere, where the only habits were our own.

On our return to normality, we moved into our first house on Lock Lane in Partington, a two-bedroom town house bought for the princely sum of £6,400 thanks to a 100 per cent mortgage from Bucklow Rural District Council.

Sylvia worked at Shell Chemicals in nearby Carrington, and by this time I'd joined the *Daily Mail* in Deansgate, Manchester, as that news sub-editor on a four-day week back then in 1975. The taste of the high life was just beginning with £84 a week wages – paid in cash – and another £36 picked up in readies working a Saturday shift on the *Sunday Mirror* on the other side of Manchester at Withy Grove.

I worked my way up the subs' desk with regular stints as the *Mail*'s splash sub, where I started at 7pm and could get late stories into the paper up to 3am in the morning. Try doing that now in this era of so-called new technology.

At the end of the earlier shifts, I'd go with the lads to the Press Club on Deansgate for a pint or three and a game of snooker. Often we'd be challenged to a game by a local Irishman, who would always wipe the floor with us. Alex Higgins was his name and world championship snooker was his game.

We did better at football. Every Maundy Thursday we'd be challenged to a match against our London office and the *Mail* would pay for a coach and a night's hotel in the capital with not a monk in sight.

I remember one match at Tottenham's training ground where we hammered our southern softies in such an embarrassing style that sports-writing icon Jeff Powell ripped his borrowed Spurs shirt off his back, threw it on the pitch and stormed off to the dressing room before the match had ended.

That set the standard for the after-match celebration in London that night, although a trick played on one of our players didn't end well. Reporter Ian Smith loved his whisky, and one of the lads thought it would be funny to nick his glass when he wasn't looking – and replace the famous gold liquid with … vinegar. Smithy slugged the glass in one and the look of horror on his face will live with me forever. He began choking, spluttering, gagging. Seemingly he was allergic to vinegar and an ambulance had to be called.

So off Smithy went for a night in hospital while we carried on celebrating in his absence. No surprise then that when he returned to join us on the coach the following day the look on his face was more than solemn.

We were soon back in Manchester and into the office for another subbing shift – and an end-of-night drink in the Press Club before returning to the new marital home.

I must admit, I drank over the limit. You did in those days. But I had the comfort of driving home with copies of that morning's newspapers on the back seat. I lost count of the number of times I'd drive down Deansgate to be met by a copper standing in the middle of the road shining a torch at my windscreen.

'Where have you been, lad?' was always the opening question after ordering me to pull over. 'Working, officer,' I'd reply. 'I'm on the *Daily Mail*.'

The torch would be switched off with never a request for a blow into the bag. 'Have you got any spare newspapers?' I'd be asked. I'd hastily fumble in the back for the *Mail* and *Daily Mirror* to keep the policeman happy as he waved me on my way.

Happy times, which were about to get very much better.

CHAPTER 4

I LOST count of the number of times I'd asked the *Daily Mail* editor Peter Clowes if I could switch to the sports desk. He always had a reason for not allowing me to fulfil my great ambition. Then one Friday he summoned me to his office and said a position on the sports desk had just come up and I could finally switch. Wow. Me and Syl had a few drinks that night to celebrate.

We had a load more the following evening too, when, after my Saturday shift on the *Sunday Mirror*, I was asked by sports editor Alan Tweedie whether I fancied a job full-time at the Manchester Withy Grove office.

Yes, yes, yes. My God. Dreams do come true. I couldn't wait to tell the *Mail*, much to Mr Clowes's annoyance, and worked the three months' notice period to the best of my ability before the *Sunday Mirror* role beckoned in earnest.

The decade-plus time I spent at Thomson House was the best journalistic period of my life. Working with colleagues and real friends in the shape of deputy sports editor Peter Shaw, who would soon step up to be boss, sports writer Vince Wilson, George Dowson, John Huxley and Billy Boy Bill Thornton. We had laughs galore. Great times aplenty, both at work and socially at Christmas, and just about any available occasion when we could get together at a bar with our better halves.

The office was vibrant. Alive with humour. That's when we were in there. A chunk of our lives was devoted to extended lunchtimes across the road at the John Willy Lees or next door at the Swan with Two Necks. Oh, and there was Sam's Chop House on a Friday where we'd meet for lunch at around 1pm and return just after tea, pushing each other down basement steps on the way back to the office before taking to our desks, desperately trying to act sober.

Occasionally, acts of mischief would be planned and plotted over copious amounts of alcohol. Like the time Billy Boy and I bought water pistols from the nearby Arndale Centre. The secretaries in the office sat outside the executives' partitioned rooms and, back then, worked feverishly on their electric typewriters. Billy Boy and I thought it would be a hilarious prank to load and fire our water pistols on to the ceiling above the head of the lovely prim and proper Wendy Dutton. The resulting water droplets would fall like rain on to her typewriter.

Wendy couldn't believe what was happening as shots of water fell on her carefully coutured hairstyle before splashing on to her electric machine. Shouts of horror followed and Wendy immediately stared at the ceiling above to check for what must be a serious leak. Without hesitation, and before we could explain, she called the maintenance office and three workers with ladders rushed to the 'rain-drenched' area of Wendy's desk. Before we knew it, they had ripped away the polystyrene tiles and continued taking down the ceiling before replacing the 'damaged' area with a new one – at a cost of £15,000.

Billy Boy and I were mortified. But in the interests of keeping our jobs, we remained tight-lipped about 'watergate', vowing never to tell Wendy the truth. Sorry Wendy.

That clearly was one gag that got out of hand. Another involved, yes you've guessed it, drink and another trip to the Arndale Centre joke shop. This time Billy Boy and Millarman spotted bags of 'sweets' on sale, but not, of course, the toffee variety. No, no. When the victims, mainly of the female variety, opened up the 'sweet', they discovered to their horror a condom lying underneath the wrapper. Screams were plentiful and laughs from me and Billy Boy in ample supply – just like the sweets.

The joke ran its natural course until one late Saturday night/Sunday morning when the final editions were printed and we retired to the office of editor Derek Dodd for a nightcap before getting taxis home.

My old pal, Bob Bayliss, who too had found a job on the *Sunday Mirror*, unearthed and unwrapped the final 'sweet' and threw the rubber at my head. I picked it up and flung the condom back at Bob, where it hit the wall and slid down behind the office fridge. We forget all about it until midway through Sunday morning when a call reached home from a not-too-happy editor.

'Steve, what the hell went on in my office last night?' said Derek. 'The cleaners were servicing my room and found a condom behind the fridge.'

Naturally I denied all knowledge, especially when the editor explained that the cleaners had immediately downed tools and gone on strike. Funny how some jokes can really backfire.

Derek was left bemused and bewildered and was even more stony-faced than usual when we returned to the office the following Tuesday. He was furious that someone had used his room for more than just a tipple.

He didn't have many light-hearted moments. In fact, his humour was non-existent, although he did make an effort to bring a smile to our faces one Christmas. Dorek Dead, as we nicknamed him, decided to remove his shoes and walk around the office in a pair of hairy, rubber gorilla feet. But I'd spotted him changing in his office so ran into the newsroom to alert every reporter and sub-editor working that December Saturday night. I told them all not to acknowledge the apish joke and to carry on as normal, which everyone did, much to Derek's bewilderment, while I removed his shoes from his office and hid them, never to be seen again.

It took some explaining from the editor to the taxi driver on the way home to Prestwich about why the boss of the *Sunday Mirror* was aping a gorilla. How lovely it would have been to have done the same all those years later to editor Piers Morgan when I worked on the *Daily Mirror*.

Anyway, back to Withy Grove and the *Sunday Mirror*, where, as I said, we worked hard and played even harder. But it's difficult not to get away from the fun factor, and one little gem came courtesy of Billy Boy back in October 1981 when Bryan Robson moved from West Brom to

Manchester United for a British record fee of £1.5m. Our sports editor Pete Shaw asked Bill to pop over to Old Trafford to interview Robbo for the forthcoming Sunday edition. Bill was delighted and off he went.

Two hours later, Billy Boy returned to the office looking as red in the face as Robbo's new shirt. Seemingly, he'd carried out the interview, and ten minutes in the interviewee turned to Bill and said, 'You don't know who I am do you?'

A blushing Bill replied, 'Yes I do. You're Bryan Robson, United's new signing.'

To which the interviewee replied, 'No, I'm not. I'm bloody Scott McGarvey.'

I still to this day don't know what was worse. Bill getting the player mixed up or actually admitting to a bunch of mickey-taking journalists his case of mistaken identity.

Billy Boy, though, was a real professional despite that confession and, like me and the rest of the *Mirror* boys, always enjoyed the job and the benefits that went with it.

Like the 'pinkies' on a Friday, where you could go to the cashiers before lunch at Sam's and get a cash advance on your expenses, which paid for the grub and booze. Or often a big money hit before heading off to sunny climes on holiday with 'pinky' bundles in hand to spend on a family fest in Jersey with Syl, and Nikky and Anthony, our gorgeous children.

Life was good – and the fun never ended. Vince was our main football writer and his contacts were impeccable and far-reaching, especially at Liverpool, where he counted the legendary Bob Paisley as a personal friend.

Vince, a staunch Sunderland fan and old next-door neighbour of Brian Clough in Middlesbrough where they babysat each other's kids, had strong north-east links with players at Burnley and Huddersfield Town. So in the summer Vince would arrange a get-together – or a day on the booze if we're describing it correctly and honestly.

This started as a few drinks in a local pub with a game of dominoes. The following year it progressed to a darts and pool competition, with the next summer being the final act after the summer ball was well and truly deflated. A pub was booked on the moors and the private lunch a big success, with the hors d'oeuvres being the arrival of stripper Lolita, who explained to a packed audience that her real name was Lorraine. Lolita was certainly a big hit with the players, who got stuck in even more to the drink on offer before negotiating the journey home to Lancashire and Yorkshire.

I really didn't expect the party to be such a big hit, though, with Huddersfield boss Mick Buxton phoning me the next day to ask what the bloody hell happened to his squad. Seemingly, four had missed training after crashing their cars into farmers' fields. Oops. However, Mick, despite me putting his star players in peril, didn't hold a grudge and we became good friends, with the Terriers' boss staying at my house after Football Writers' Dinners in Manchester.

I was privileged, too, to spend time in the company of Cloughie, who was a columnist for the *Sunday Mirror* with Vince his ghost writer.

It was back in September 1985 when Vince was going on holiday and he and sports editor Peter asked me whether I'd stand in to interview the legend that was, after England played Romania at Wembley. The 'yes' reply came faster than a machine gun bullet.

Vince advised me to introduce myself to Cloughie the week before to touch base and arrange a meeting. So I phoned Nottingham Forest and Carol his secretary asked me to be at the ground at 6.30pm before they played a league match.

No excuse, I know, but the traffic was terrible. And with no sat nav in those days I also got lost in Nottingham, arriving at the City Ground at 7pm – 30 minutes before kick-off. I introduced myself to Carol, who told me to wait outside the manager's office, with a warning that he wouldn't be best pleased.

At around 7.20pm Brian marched towards me in the corridor and gave me a huge rollicking for not being on time. With that he urged me into his office and poured a huge whisky for himself and me before outlining the Wembley plans. I can remember him saying, 'I'm doing TV that night so meet me after the game in the Aberdeen Angus Steakhouse down Wembley way. My directors will be there and you can dine with them. Then we will sit down and do the piece on my England verdict.'

Cloughie, still in charge of Forest despite decade-long links with the England job, left with minutes to spare until kick-off. I finished the Scotch alone in his office before watching the maestro in action in the dugout.

The following Wednesday I travelled to Wembley to witness a shocking 1-1 draw, and after the final whistle walked over to the Aberdeen Angus Steakhouse. Sure enough, the directors arrived and I was duly entertained as Cloughie's guest.

No sign of the great man as the hours ticked by. Then just past midnight Cloughie appeared through the restaurant door and ordered the chairman and directors to the waiting coach. I couldn't believe it. What about my interview? What about our three pages to fill on Sunday? I just stared at Cloughie and said, 'What about our story, Brian?'

'Son, I've not got time. The TV debate went on longer than I thought. But hey, here's the intro for your story on Sunday. This was the night I knew I never wanted to be the England boss. Now, phone Carol in the morning. She'll put you through to my office and we'll take it from there and do the interview over the phone.'

Yes Mr Clough.

My respect for the greatest manager England never had, had no limits. So in his sad latter years, when I was on the *Daily Mirror*, a story came out of the Midlands that he'd fallen drunk into a ditch near his home. I was sent to get the full story but, really, I didn't have the heart to further expose a legend in his hours of need. I dutifully found his house and looked through the window. Brian was asleep in the lounge chair, looking frail and unwell. I wasn't going to disturb the great man, so I phoned the office to say there was no sign of Brian Clough at his home. It was an easy call to make.

Brian was right up there on the list of my all-time heroes. Another was Liverpool legend Bob Paisley. I remember one summer being sent to Malton, North Yorkshire, where Bob loved to spend a week at the stables of his trainer friend Frankie Carr. The feature and photographs couldn't have been any more dramatic.

Here was the winner of three European Cups and six league titles happily rolling his sleeves up and sweeping the straw and sh** out of the yards. Can you imagine anyone else getting that down and dirty when you were manager of one of the greatest club sides in history?

But that was Bob. A hero and legend of the Kop but at heart just an ordinary guy from the small County Durham coal mining village of Hetton-le-Hole, where his father Sam was a miner and his mother Emily a housewife.

I was also privileged to visit his bungalow in Woolton, Liverpool, to get the Bob Paisley big match verdict for the *Sunday Mirror* on a couple of FA Cup Finals at Wembley. The first time was a real eye-opener. I knocked on his door, with a bottle of champagne proudly displayed in my arms, only for Bob to open and stare at the offered Moët.

'I don't drink that stuff,' he said. 'If you're coming again bring a couple of bottles of Guinness.' Which I duly did.

On both occasions it was an eye-opener to watch the Wembley final sat alongside him on the couch while his wife Jessie hand-mowed the lawn in the summer heat. His knowledge of the game showed no bounds. But what was more amazing was his eye for injury. Bob had originally joined Liverpool's back room as a self-taught physiotherapist and could diagnose a player's injury just by looking at them. While we watched his TV, he'd prove the point by saying such and such was struggling. Five minutes later they would hit the deck and be helped off the pitch.

My journalistic life was awesome – and it wasn't bad away from the game's greats and the stadia around the north-west of England where football in the 70s and 80s flourished.

My sports editor Pete Shaw played a big part in my and Sylvia's early decision about where to live with our growing girl Nikky and baby Anthony. Life in Lock Lane, Partington, was great but we needed a bigger house and we sold for £6,800, making a handsome £400 profit.

So where to go? Well, we stumbled across the Warrington area of Woolston, Cheshire, and decided to buy a newly built semi-detached just off Manchester Road for £10,995. I remember one day in the office telling Pete of our plans and he stopped me mid-sentence. He told me to push myself financially to the limits and the cash reward would follow down the line.

We did break the bank – not for the first time in our lives – and in March 1978 invested £12,995 in a gorgeous detached in Hereford Close, which became our lovely family home until we moved again as the kids got older. This time we really climbed up the ladder, with the purchase of a palatial four-bedroom detached in Redwood Close for £49,995 just before Christmas in 1985.

It was onwards and upwards in every walk of life, both professionally and domestically, with my journalistic experience now growing with reports on First Division matches on a Saturday for the *Sunday Mirror*.

This is the time in my life where I started to meet and get pally with players of the time, with Manchester City's Peter Barnes, Gary Owen and Asa Hartford good drinking buddies after a Saturday night match. I was living the dream at home and at work with the Blue connection gaining even more strength. I'd been a City fan from afar on those RAF camps and would really look forward to Christmas and Easter holidays when the Millars would descend on Mum's family in Chorlton-cum-Hardy, Manchester.

I remember cycling one day to the old Maine Road and standing outside the main entrance where a giant of a man appeared from the players' entrance. It was 'Mr goalkeeping', the legend himself, Bert Trautmann, who beckoned the shy starstruck lad over.

'Here's half a crown, son,' he said. 'Can you run over to the butcher's shop and get me two pork pies?' Which I did, of course, without hesitation. I can still feel the warmth from the brown paper bag as I placed the pastries into his huge bucket-like hands with a grateful Mr Trautmann telling me to keep the shilling change. I was rich in money and memories.

I can also recall vividly another magical moment when I was at a Boxing Day match with my dad, granddad Jack Robinson and uncle Harry Havery, a plumber who, it was always said, was lined up to sign for City before breaking his leg in his last match for Wolverhampton Wanderers. Maine Road was jammed to capacity and us kids were handed down above the fans' heads to sit on the pitchside wall.

So there I perched, keeping check of the time played by constantly glancing at my wrist, now adorned by a huge, framed gold watch my dad had purchased from an Arab trader before leaving Aden. The fake jewelled timepiece was unmissable, particularly when another City legend Johnny Crossan trotted near me to retrieve the ball for a throw-in.

Johnny spotted the watch and said, 'How long left, son?'

I stammered a reply: 'Two minutes, Mr Crossan.' God, I was chuffed that I helped a City great to see out the match for a rare victory.

Fast forward 30-odd years and here I was in the company of Barnes and co. continuing my City education with greats of the Blue Moon fraternity.

But my life was to take another turn when, out of the blue so to speak, we were sent letters in the May of 1988 that *Mirror* owner Robert Maxwell had made a no-going-back decision. Maxwell had promised us when he turned Withy Grove into his new technology newspaper hub that Manchester was going to be the epicentre of his publishing world. And we believed him, more fool us, as every Saturday we'd travel to the London office by train while Withy Grove was fitted with the latest in computer wizardry. That lasted 18 months.

It was me, Pete Shaw and Billy Boy who made the weekly journey, with tickets that also included drinks vouchers, which we could swap for whisky, gin and vodka miniatures for the midnight sleeper back to Manchester. Our sleeper attendant was always Brian, or 'fried egg' as we used to call him, as he was as tall as he was wide. Five foot either way. He was brilliant and brought our drinks to our sleeping compartments once the train had glided out of Euston.

God, we had fun and frolics. Joined a few times by some of the *Coronation Street* cast, who were invited in for a free drink from hospitable journalists. Sometimes, well most times, the noise levels grew to party level, which didn't always go down too well with fellow 'sleepers'.

I remember once, about an hour into the journey, there came a furious knock on my compartment door. I opened to see a livid Frank Finlay standing in front of me in baggy string vest and underpants, screaming for the eight of us inside to turn the noise down. The legend of stage and TV with *Casanova* to his credits, ranted until I told him politely to exit stage left with a final message: 'Call yourself Casanova? In those Y-fronts?'

All that fun ended with those Mirror Group letters of dismissal. The northern offices, which were our second home, were to close forever. The end of an incredible era.

I was offered a job as sports assistant editor in London and even received an official letter of appointment from editor Eve Pollard. But I wouldn't entertain that move. I had great family and friends in the good old north and certainly didn't want to uproot Syl and the kids to move down south.

Any worries about my immediate future were declared null and void when I received a phone call from former *Daily Star* founder Peter Grimsditch. Would I be interested in being sports editor of the soon-to-be-launched *Daily Sport* in Manchester? That, as they say, was a no-brainer.

But I can't leave the *Sunday Mirror* chapter without one final memory from so many, which literally flies in the face of all that frivolity we enjoyed in Thomson House.

Every May, Billy Boy and I would jet off to Belfast for the Northern Ireland Footballer of the Year awards. But one trip scared the lives out of both of us. We boarded the plane at Liverpool Airport, not realising we were due to land at the Isle of Man to pick up more passengers. I wasn't the best flyer in the world and wasn't happy when I found out about the scheduled stop.

Anyway, land in the Isle of Man we did. Got the passengers on board and slowly made our way to the start of the runway. The engines roared and off we went – only for the take-off to be aborted at the last possible minute. The captain explained that a light aircraft had crossed his path just as he was about to leave God's earth and the plane skidded and skewed to a halt, throwing us head-first into the seats in front.

I didn't listen much to the captain's calming address. I just wanted off that plane and beckoned a stewardess. I told her I was leaving and she went to speak to the captain before returning to tell me and Billy Boy that we could exit the plane. However, she said we must leave quietly and retrieve our luggage from the hold, which we did, courtesy of baggage handlers. So we struggled across the tarmac with our cases and golf bags, disappointed we couldn't enjoy a round with our colleague Bill Clark at Helen's Bay Golf Club the following day.

We were relieved, though, to get off that bloody plane and headed for the terminal door, only to be surrounded by armed police and security. It was the time of the Troubles and they were highly suspicious of two guys getting off a Belfast-bound plane.

CHAPTER 4

Two hours later they were satisfied we were frightened out of our lives … well I was. They let us out of the airport and we took a taxi into Douglas, booked into a hotel, played golf the next day – and got a ticket back to Liverpool on the ferry.

That was just the start of enjoying a ride on another crest of a wave.

CHAPTER 5

MY *DAILY SPORT* career began with a breakfast meeting with Peter 'Grimbles' Grimsditch at a hotel near Manchester Airport. The editor impressed me with his enthusiasm, his vision and his commitment to this new venture of launching a national newspaper from scratch. There was me, Peter and his former *Daily Star* secretary Christine Turkentine. That's all. Three amigos with a shared love of being at the start of something new.

We'd all had extensive careers on established newspapers and here we were in the April of 1988, working hard and enthusiastically to hit Fleet Street with a publication we believed would be a major success.

Peter downed endless mugs of coffee on the hotel terrace as he explained how the new *Daily Sport* would hit the paper shops running. We were owned by *Sunday Sport* publisher David Sullivan but the new paper would distance itself from the 'World War Two Bomber Found on Moon' sister publication. We were to be just like his old paper, the *Daily Star*. If that was mainly in the gutter, then we'd exist below that. There would be topless girls, for sure, and many of them, posted throughout the paper instead of just a solitary pose on page 3.

There would be fun stories and serious ones from the day's events, too. And the edict was that sport would attempt to compete with all competitors on the market, such as the *Daily Mirror*, *Star* and *Sun*. A fourth red top with an ambition to compete on the highly competitive sporting front.

But first the *Daily Sport* had to start from humble beginnings. Peter had rented a cottage in Mossley, in the foothills of the Pennines, close to Oldham. There he and Christine worked tirelessly to set the wheels in motion towards the birth of the one-day-a-week *Daily Sport* by August.

I was asked to start a news and sports library where I, Nikky and Anthony busied ourselves with cutting out the stories from the day's national newspapers and filing them into folders. It was laborious but good fun too, as our lounge carpet became littered with cuttings.

Phone calls from Peter were frequent – and long. He had meetings coming out of his ears with Sullivan and the three publishing centres we'd use come August. In Bradford at the *Telegraph and Argus* offices, in Kettering and Burgess Hill in Sussex.

They were exciting times, to be such an integral part of something new. Peter and I would meet in various Manchester pubs for updates on the countdown to the launch. The looks from fellow customers were always ones of curiosity, to see two suited and booted gents walk into their establishment with Peter carrying a mobile phone the size of a medium suitcase.

It wasn't long before Peter and Christine found our first home, St James' House in Salford, a few miles from Manchester. The new *Daily Sport* office occupied the first floor and one by one the number of staff grew from the three founders. We all worked tirelessly as the days counted down to the August launch, with a weekly Wednesday edition occupying all our thoughts.

One day we had a visitor the few of us present in the office will never forget. David Sullivan had phoned to say that his new managing director would be driving up to Salford from London – one late-teens Karren Brady, whose dad, we were told, was a close friend of our owner.

Ms Brady duly walked into the office, obviously unaware of who anyone was. She unashamedly went to each desk and asked the occupant, 'And what do you do?' That lack of a briefing about the new *Daily Sport* team didn't go down well and the expletives could be heard echoing around St James' House.

That wasn't my first and only brush with Ms Brady. Many months later when we were in full production she phoned me to ask whether I could get a photograph of Ryan Giggs blown up and posted to her for framing. Seemingly, she was a Giggsy worshipper and wanted him on her wall.

I arranged this favour with the picture desk and thought no more about the request until a rude phone call from Ms Brady while I was playing golf. I wasn't aware that the photo had become a Ryangate affair with news of her love for the Welsh hero handed exclusively to *Private Eye*. Ms Brady blamed me for the Welsh leak and threatened yours truly with the sack, until I managed to convince her in the end that this sports editor was not guilty. We didn't have much dealings after that, I'm delighted to recall, as the *Daily Sport* was up and running.

It was hard work with long hours for just publishing on a Wednesday at first. But there was plenty of relaxation as well with daily 'lunches' in the curiously named Flat Iron pub on Salford Precinct. There were characters in there, I can tell you. And from the start we made an impression with scenes straight out of the TV cult show *Shameless*.

The editorial staff of four would walk in suited and booted, and the minute we entered, the locals would dart for the exits, believing we were CID. They stayed in their seats when they got used to the idea that the suspicious-looking guys on the next table were journalists.

It was a mad time and launch day came with a night of real euphoria in Bradford, where a limited drink was taken before driving back home to the Millar abode in Woolston, Warrington. We were off and running.

The *Daily Sport* was selling above 200,000 copies, one day a week, and within a year the growing editorial team relocated to Ancoats in Manchester, where good old Peter had shaken hands on a deal to rent the old *Express* offices and printing plant.

The next stage of development was for the *Daily Sport* to be published for a second and third day before the switch to a full six-day operation in 1991. And in that time I formed what was to me one of the best and most talented sports desk teams in the history of Fleet Street.

I'd first appointed my old *Sunday Mirror* colleague George Dowson as my number two but he only lasted a few weeks before quitting because he couldn't admit to his strict Roman Catholic family that he was working for such a sex-based newspaper. So that gave me the opportunity to appoint the man of *The People*, Phil Smith, who revelled in the role of deputy sports editor on such a flirtatious publication. It was an honour to have Phil alongside me, with his journalistic experience the envy of every other newspaper.

The writing team was strong from day one, with Alan Nixon providing the *Daily Sport*'s first back-page splash on that wonderful opening Wednesday. Old Billy Boy worked for us for a time and Tim Taylor also joined the team as senior sports reporter before Dave Maddock took his seat.

Tim was *Express* old school and great at his job, also ghosting a Saturday column with football legend and pal of ours Malcolm Macdonald, who I'm still a friend of today. His column was brilliant, which still makes me wonder why our rival newspapers never spoke to him, never mind grab him on board as a great columnist.

I billed Tim throughout the sports pages as 'Tim Taylor, the Man with Clout'. However, one day, when he said he was suffering from ankle pain and struggling to walk, that changed to 'Man with Gout'. He also foolishly admitted that he was a bit short of money and asked whether he could have a pay rise. The next day it was Tim Taylor, the 'Man with Nowt'.

We also had a few cod names running across other sports. Our fishing column was written by Dan Dangle, and Wimbledon every year was covered by Annette Court. But my all-time favourite was the Dubai classic golf, where our correspondent filed under the name of Mustapha Putt.

We certainly brought a smile to faces of our readers, and those in the office, where the ranks were filled with such formidable journalists as Phil Thomas, Janine Self, Julie Stott, Carl Hall, Keith Meadows and number three on the desk, Bill Woodcock, or 'Timber tool' as he was affectionately known.

Oh, and I'll always remember the day I received a package from a young journalist on a local paper around Crewe and Sandbach, filled with feature cuttings and news stories. He wanted to be given a chance on a national newspaper, so without an interview, as was my practice in those heady days, Andy Dunn, now billed by the *Mirror* as the newspaper's best columnist, became part of our terrific team.

Our racing desk was furlongs ahead of other specialist teams on rival newspapers in my opinion, with Keith Hamer and Peter Levy at the reins and producing brilliant pages. There was also Graham Nickless in the south and, for a wonderful while, dear old Peter Batt. Ted Corbett and his wife Jo King (yes really) covered the cricket and Ted Macauley took care of the motor racing. Professionals with a capital 'P', supported financially by generous owners who paid good salaries – until the financial walls came tumbling down.

We were able to send Tim Taylor to the 1990 World Cup in Italy, and Phil Thomas flew out to Australia in 1992 to cover the Great Britain Rugby League tour. Thanks still, Mr Sullivan. Yes, the millionaire owner loved his sport and always delivered a fax every morning listing his footballing ideas for the day, some of which worked. I didn't mind that, although phone calls from his bubbling jacuzzi with Page 3 model voices in the background were a bit disconcerting.

Sullivan knew what he wanted – and knew what he didn't want. Like never reporting a red card if issued by the referee for any of his players at Birmingham, the club he'd just bought with David Gold. And we were instructed to always refer to his players in match reports as £2m-rated or £1m-rated. Yes, different days.

I was free, though, to report unbiased for the *Sunday Mirror* on Saturday's matches on a freelance basis before the *Daily Sport* sprung into full-time action.

It's with a deep dread that I recount in horror that April day in 1989 when I drove to Hillsborough to report on the FA Cup semi-final between Liverpool and Nottingham Forest, alongside the *Sunday Mirror*'s chief football writer, good old Scot Ken Montgomery. A day that will vividly live with me forever.

The journey from my Warrington home to the stadium across the Pennines was arduous to say the least. And as soon as I dropped down to Hillsborough from the Woodhead Pass I sensed danger. I couldn't believe that Forest fans had been allocated the larger stand behind the goal and Liverpool the fateful Leppings Lane end. Cars and coaches from the Woodhead had to crawl past the Forest end to find parking at the opposite, crowded area of the stadium. Forest supporters coming from their M1 direction had to inch their way past the

Leppings Lane end to reach their own parking spots. Bloody mayhem.

I was late. Very late. But I eventually jammed my car into a small space on a housing estate high above the Leppings Lane end. I ran, panicking, past pubs still packed with Liverpool fans and glanced at my watch. Twenty to three. Why were all these supporters not supping their pints and heading off to the ground, still some 300 yards away? Why weren't they on the terraces eating their hot dogs and getting ready for the match?

I passed the Leppings Lane five minutes later and was wide-eyed at the hundreds bunched into the tight entrance, jostling to get through the turnstiles. My immediate and now life-lasting thought was: *Thank God I'm not going into Hillsborough from there.*

I eventually took my seat in the overflow press box just as the game kicked off and noticed immediately that Forest VIP fans in front of me were worse the wear for alcohol as well. They were also abusive and threatening.

The whole, packed stadium was shrouded in an unnerving mood, with my attention caught by Liverpool supporters behind Bruce Grobbelaar's goal. They were enclosed, of course, by high fencing erected in those hooligan days and some were squeezing their arms through the metal gaps, pleading for help to escape their overcrowding hell. I could see many pressed against the fencing and they were begging police to open the emergency gates to ease the life-threatening pressure. The cops looked. Dismissed them as hooligans. Turned their backs.

I remember Bruce furiously trying to attract the attention of stewards and match officials but nothing was done until the match was halted at 3.06pm.

And then the full horror unfolded. We all stood there helpless as fans desperately attempted to scramble over the fencing. Others were dragged up to the safety of the higher stand by fellow supporters offering their arms as lifelines.

My mind's eye will never erase the sight of lifeless bodies sprawled in front of our stand, with fellow Koppites desperately trying to revive them with hand pumps to their chests. Others were carried away to the exits on advertising hoardings as the one ambulance in attendance mysteriously never drove on to the pitch. Life-saving equipment, though, was limited to say the least, with one steward admitting to me some time later that the oxygen tanks beneath the main stand were empty.

There were so many scenes of horror that you wondered immediately how many fans were dying. The FA first reported about an hour later that six had perished. But that figure was widely off the mark even then.

I followed up reports that Liverpool fans had forced a metal door off its runner to gain entry and spoke to a fire brigade official. First he confirmed that the door hadn't been forced and then asked what the early official death toll was. I told him six and he just looked at me solemnly, admitting that behind the Leppings Lane door we were standing by were at least 40 bodies.

I was stunned. Still am. Still can't believe that the final fatality figures would rise to 96 on a day when supporters went to a game of football and never came home.

I don't know how I got through the day, reporting to copy takers in London after queuing for the one available phone in the press box. And then staying in Sheffield for the police press conference in the evening, with no contact with my own family to tell them I was safe. A nightmare then and a nightmare now, with an abiding feeling that even today I'm not comfortable in crowds. Hate to be jostled.

Writing about my inner feelings again for my own paper was a harrowing experience but one that had to be done as I recounted seeing bodies lying side by side in the Hillsborough gym.

My life, luckily, went on, with the madness of working on the *Sport* giving me back my focus. We were going from strength to strength with even my daughter Nikky and her friend Kerry enlisted as Sunday casual workers. They would answer phones. Open filthy letters from many of the unsavoury readers. Send off posters and knickers of a Page 3 girl called Fiona to perverts up and down the land. But in return they got £50 a day – a decent cash payment for seeing how I made a very good living.

It was good to get up in the morning and drive to the *Daily Sport* office. I always looked forward to the day's colourful events and ending the shift in the curiously named Land O' Cakes pub across the road.

We had a ball, literally. Although there was a sinister twist to life as a sports editor after Big Tim and I ran a story about the highly intimidating atmosphere at Elland Road. A cauldron of hate we branded the Leeds United stadium.

I thought no more about it until a few days later when my sports desk secretary Helen opened a letter with a Leeds postmark and straight out of a murder mystery episode on the telly. Separate words had been cut out of newspapers to spell out the bone-chilling message that my life was in danger: 'We know where you live and when you're driving home at night look in your wing mirror. We will be behind you.'

My God. A death threat or what? I went straight to the police station behind the Ancoats office and showed the desk sergeant. He was horrified too and called two detectives, who interviewed me. I was promised a police 'shadow' for the next couple of nights when driving home. I never saw my cop minders or any Leeds nutters either. But for a couple of weeks I was extremely concerned for the safety of myself, Syl and the kids.

Back to reality and normality, though. The *Daily Sport* was growing in strength and circulation, but after editor Peter Grimsditch left, the office atmosphere changed and the editorial balance shifted. Clueless staff from the *Sunday Sport* were moved into our department and I was effectively shoved to one side, my sports editor duty relinquished.

I wasn't happy at losing my position and decided to move on, too, to form a freelance agency with my mate Alan Nixon called Premier Sport, where we worked exclusively for *Sunday Mirror* sports editor Dave Balmforth after shaking hands on a deal.

Big Al and I loved every minute of our six months in business together, amassing a cool £60,000 in that short period until Dave phoned early one morning to say he'd just been appointed *Daily Mirror* sports editor. Dave wanted me to work for him – but not with Premier Sport. He said it would be cheaper to give me a full-time job on the paper.

I agreed. And the next chapter in my journalistic life began with a magnificent six-year career, rocketing Steve Millar to another level.

CHAPTER 6

I MUST admit I was nervous in joining the *Mirror* as their Northern Sports Writer. Sure, I had donkey's years of experience in the job but sports reporting on the front line of a national newspaper was a daunting prospect. I'd always had a mix of journalistic roles on my other papers, so writing full-time on football, golf, cricket, etc. was a whole new ball game.

But I couldn't have got off to a better start back when Millarman became Mirrorman in 1993. The year before I was still shifting on a Saturday for sister paper the *Sunday Mirror* and was sent to Boundary Park for Oldham's First Division clash with Leeds United in the February. Nothing significant about that fixture, you might argue, but how wrong could you be?

The Leeds dugout before the match was mobbed by photographers trying to snap what would be the phenomenon of English football – Eric Cantona. The fabulous Frenchman had joined the Elland Road club for £1m the previous month and he came on to make his debut as a substitute in a 2-0 defeat at Oldham.

I remember vividly the clamour of pressmen trying to grab 'Le King' for a post-match interview. I was lucky. I knew Boundary Park like the back of my hand and knew also that the players never returned to the pitch to give interviews. The players' lounge was where they would be before heading home, so I found myself mingling with the drinking fans before catching sight of Eric. I approached him and he didn't back off. Told me in broken English how delighted he was to be in England as he sang the praises of Leeds United.

What struck me instantly was what a genuine guy he was. No airs. No graces. No aloofness. No big-time Charlie with Eric. Here was a magnificent man of stature, yes, but never any 'Billy Big Time' aura about him.

Eric lived with first wife Isabelle and their two children in a modest semi-detached on the outskirts of Leeds, a house I'd found and chatted at the door to Mrs Cantona, a shy, quiet lovely lady. So I had enough of an in, as they say, to be recognised by 'Le King' after he joined Manchester United for £1.2m in November 1992.

I remember a couple of matches into his United career he gave me an exclusive interview pitchside at Old Trafford, much to the annoyance of my fellow scribes on the Manchester beat. *The Sun*'s Peter Fitton, and David Walker from the *Daily Mail* had intentionally blanked the new bloke on the block. But seeing from a distance my love affair with Eric, I was quickly invited into their circle to share regular quotes from one of United's greatest-ever players.

Suddenly, I was everyone's companion and life was great as I settled into my new, if not daunting, role. I soon met and introduced myself to United's star playing cast, including Steve Bruce, Bryan Robson, Gary Pallister and co. And, oh yes, I nearly forgot, Sir Alex.

In fact, my relationship with Brucie and Robbo was enriched by a chance meeting with the dynamic duo at the Four Seasons luxury apartment complex in Vilamoura, Portugal, in the summer of '93.

My old mucker Peter Barnes had a connection to the resort, along with his dad, City's former great and chief scout Ken. Sylvia, Anthony and I were booked into a lovely little villa for a ridiculous £50 for the week. It was strange at first, holidaying without Nikky, who as a teenager was living it up with her girlfriends in some Balearic island. We'd always spent hols together, with America a regular haunt due to endless accommodation offers throughout the States courtesy of Auntie Hilda and Uncle Gene.

Mind you, one trip to Florida still haunts me to this day. We were lapping up the wonders of Disney World until one day, at the Wet 'N' Wild water theme park, when Syl and I were facing the ultimate horror of having our baby girl kidnapped. Nikky had wanted to buy a wacky American type of ice cream and asked for a dollar to get one at a kiosk behind a hedge where we had our sun-beds. She skipped off excitedly and we waited for her return.

And waited and waited. No Nikky. We both thought she was queuing for the iced treat and went to the kiosk. No Nikky. Christ, she's not there – a horrific scenario manifested, not helped by having watched on TV the night before the growing trend of kidnapping from Disney parks. When a case is reported all the gates go on lockdown and the traumatised parents wait at the one-and-only exit to spot their child. But by then the kidnappers have cut the child's hair and dressed him or her in different clothes.

Syl ran hysterically to the missing children's office and reported that Nikky had vanished. We both just looked at each other with scary eyes, picturing the scene of flying home to England with an empty seat on the plane.

That feeling of devastating, horrific loss lasted for ten minutes. A timeline of dread and family destruction – until Nikky suddenly came walking towards us, smiling, with her ice cream treat being devoured.

Boy, did she get a roasting – and an emotional embrace – with our daughter explaining to two blubbering wrecks that the first kiosk man didn't have any of her new favourites left and had sent her across the park to another vendor. Idiot man.

It all ended with tears and eventual laughter, but we still worried about her all those years later on that separate holiday, with our own seven-day break being not quite as eventful but memorable to say the least.

Our first night at the Vilamoura bar saw the shock arrival of Brucie, Robbo and their families, who had booked into the Four Seasons for their own holiday break. The United legends both looked at me over the top of their lager pints and approached.

'What happens here, stays here,' they both echoed. And, as you did in those days, my word of non-disclosure was accepted. They trusted me – and still do.

Robbo was so honest in revealing to me after his seventh beer how sad he'd been to pack in his England career two years earlier after 90 appearances for the Three Lions and 26 goals. He felt he'd been forced to quit his international era too soon. He loved to chat, especially with close pal Brucie as they were often locked away in their own football world.

So much so that one day around the pool they were engrossed in conversation and didn't notice Bryan's young son Ben being chucked by kids into the water for a laugh. He clearly couldn't swim and began floundering, waving his arms for help. Dad and Brucie were still reminiscing about the great old days and didn't notice Ben was in trouble. I did and dived into the pool to pull the youngster to safety – much to the relief of dad, and mum Denise.

A moment remembered so clearly by me, Robbo and Brucie, who every time he saw me after that when he was a player and manager always introduced me as the hero who saved his own son Alex. Funny, the effects of strong lager. I've never corrected him ever since. Didn't have to really. Brucie, and Robbo it goes without saying, were so helpful in the years following Vilamoura with interviews as footie stars in their own successful right and as managers.

It was a privilege to be in their company, with Brucie, I recall, letting me hold his FA Cup winner's medal after United hammered Chelsea 4-0 in May 1994, with King Eric scoring twice. I was in footballing heaven – and it could only get better.

To say I had an eventful time covering United was the understatement of the century. The people I met still leave me shaking my head to this day. For instance, I became close to the Russian football agent Grigory Essaoulenko, who represented United wing star Andrei Kanchelskis and who wanted to get his player away from Old Trafford asap. Mr Essaoulenko began his exit campaign before the end of the 1994/95 season and used me to write exclusives about other clubs' interests, including his next one, Everton.

'The Bearded One', he dubbed my good self, with a request to phone him on his mobile in Moscow to keep him updated on any transfer news. I lost count of the number of times he said he was driving past the Kremlin when I reached him on his mobile. I often wondered whether he was driving there to down vodka with infamous oligarchs, such were his Russian connections.

He was certainly not a man to question – or anger. It was widely reported that Mr Essaoulenko threatened United chairman Martin Edwards in the heat of the Kanchelskis battle with the chilling words: 'If you don't transfer him now you will not be around much longer.' And Sir Alex later revealed that he was given a gift by the Russian at a Manchester hotel to sweeten the United boss and encourage him to push through that Everton deal. Fergie thought at first it was a tea urn, but to his astonishment opened up the bag to discover around £40,000 in cash notes. The Bearded One wasn't offered such monetary gifts but was nonetheless rich in exclusives from Mr Essaoulenko.

Martin Edwards was left ashen-faced by that Cold War with the Russian and was happy to sanction the Kanchelskis Goodison move for a cool £5m. Edwards was, of course, the money man of Old Trafford, who would ring me up to have a go if he didn't like that morning's *Mirror* story from my good self. He said on one occasion, 'That bloody article has cost my club £2 million.'

I reminded him instantly that he never phoned to thank me for putting £3m on the club's value when I'd written a positive piece. But to be fair, we had a great relationship. Still do, and we enjoyed many a drink or two on European trips, with Martin always asking for a favour in getting his brother Rodger back to the hotel in a taxi.

These trips were many and varied, with the first one a memorable trip in September 1995 to Russia with no Mr Essaoulenko in sight, much to the manager's and chairman's relief. United had been drawn away in the UEFA Cup to Rotor Volgograd, formerly Stalingrad. The flight was long and laborious and we arrived in the early hours to collect our bags from a Nissen hut of an arrival hall.

I was aware of Peter Fitton and David Walker in deep conversation with Sir Alex at the far end of the hut, with the United manager nodding his head before walking towards me.

Sir Alex approached, smiled and said, 'I understand you view the world through sky-blue eyes.' A reference, of course, to my Manchester City allegiance, which obviously had been disclosed by my two colleagues. That love for the 'enemy' camp was never an obstacle in our relationship, though. In fact, the banter through the years led to some magical moments between manager and journalist.

We enjoyed laughs galore – and many clips around the back of the head for yours truly when Sir Alex would arrive for his weekly press conference and target me on the way to his desk. All playful stuff and good banter.

But there were many occasions when the atmosphere wasn't so light-hearted. We had furious bust-ups, some bordering on the point of violence. But Sir Alex always forgave without forgetting. I remember vividly the day when I phoned him in his car in my early *Mirror* days to say that the relationship between manager and the media wasn't at its best. How could we build bridges? How could we improve our daily working ways? On behalf of the other lads, I suggested we meet for lunch and Sir Alex agreed, with a request that we went to his favourite hotel, Etrop Grange, just the other side of the runway at Manchester Airport.

We all put our point of view to Sir Alex over lunch and red wine and we shook hands, parting on the best of company. Very positive, I thought. Good to build bridges, which were seriously swept away the following week at an Old Trafford press conference to unveil a new 'Fergie video'.

Through contacts at Granada TV, I'd managed to obtain a copy, and on the morning of the lavish launch I'd filled three pages of *Mirror* sport with some of its best content. I was naturally nervous walking into the stadium suite and feared the worst when Sir Alex and Martin Edwards entered the room, pointing daggers in my direction as I tried not to be noticed against the wall.

Sir Alex, with TV cameras whirring, opened the press conference by saying that he couldn't believe what he'd read that morning. 'It was only last week,' he said, 'that that man over there, the man from the *Mirror*, asked me if we could build bridges. And now in one swoop he's wrecked what was to be a new relationship between me and him and the press.' Serious sentiments echoed by Mr Edwards, who jabbed an accusing finger at me, saying I'd ruined 'what should have been a day of celebration'.

I shuddered as I tried to melt into the action photographed-lined walls. But there was no hiding place. All eyes were on me and, as they say, if looks could kill… Still, I had a job to do and was determined not to walk out. I'd test the heated temperature and ask whether I could take my place on the media table to interview the great man about his video. Christ.

Just in case, I pulled our photographer Dennis Hussey to one side and told him to be ready to snap a picture of Sir Alex taking a swipe at the Millarman. I feared the worst. Sir Alex approached me, red-faced and angry-looking. But I only had to duck his vitriol and not his fists as he gave me another almighty rollicking before telling me to take my place at the table. Phew.

I recall at the end he informed me I'd be banned from his press conferences for a couple of weeks. Tough action but nowhere near as punishing as my next bust-up with the boss.

The mum and dad of a little boy with leukaemia had phoned me in the office to ask whether I could get a United shirt signed by the squad to raise money at an auction for Christie's Hospital. I agreed, collected the shirt and it stayed in my car boot for an eternity before the family reminded me they needed it back for this particular Saturday night fundraiser.

So, on the Tuesday before United played Juventus in a crucial Champions League fixture 24 hours later, I drove to the club's old training ground, The Cliff, to drop the shirt off as agreed by Sir Alex. I knocked on the iron gates, with the souvenir shirt in a carrier bag, to be greeted by a steward I knew, Harold Wood, who had first spotted Ryan Giggs on nearby pitches as a kid and got Sir Alex to watch him.

Harold told me to go straight to reception and hand the bag over. I was reluctant as the squad was training on The Cliff pitch and I didn't want to risk a 'spying' charge. But Harold insisted, so I walked across the car park purposely not gazing to my left towards the action.

I was a few yards away from the reception doors when to my complete horror the worst possible scene unfolded before my disbelieving eyes. Around the corner came Sir Alex and physio David Fevre, supporting a crocked Roy Keane, who was heavily limping towards me and the doorway.

Sir Alex looked at me, dropped his supportive arm from around his captain and ran towards me screaming, 'Millar, you're a snoop.' Well, that's the polite quote for any kids reading.

In response I dropped the bag holding the replica shirt, again waiting for fisticuffs. I shouted an explanation that it was for a boy with leukaemia to raise money at a charity auction. I further promised not to report a word on Keane being a Champions League crock and being ruled out of the Juve match. It didn't make any difference. Sir Alex was purple-faced and barked the question of who had let me in.

'Harold,' I told him.

'Right,' he screamed. 'Harold, you're fired, and Millar, you're banned.'

I left in haste and exited the training ground, leaving Sir Alex to cool down before picking up the bag and getting all his squad to sign the shirt for the charity night. He wouldn't take my call the following week to thank him. Instead, I was informed by club secretary Ken Ramsden that I was banned indefinitely, although the suspension lasted just two months.

When I returned to the fold, nothing was ever mentioned and our relationship was outstanding from then to the day I left the *Mirror* in 1999 when Syl and I took over as the new landlords of The Antelope Inn in Congleton, Cheshire.

A few weeks into my new role on the other side of the bar, I received a message from Ken Ramsden saying that Sir Alex wanted to see me after his Friday press conference. I was delighted to accept the invitation, knowing that I wouldn't be banned or maimed by the great man. So there I stood in the reception at Carrington, with Sir Alex bounding down the circular stairway to give me a huge hug in front of the disbelieving media pack. He invited me in and afterwards took me up to his office for a drink – and advice.

'Now, look son,' he said. 'You know I had a couple of pubs in Glasgow, so here's some advice. Keep your beer lines clean and don't trust the cleaners. I had one who smuggled two bottles of whisky out of the pub in a pram underneath her sleeping baby. They're all cheating b*****ds.' Christ, here I was embarking on a new career and he was still telling me how to do my job. God love him.

I'm still smiling now as I recall our time together in those memorable 90s. On one occasion we were flying to Spain, I think, and Nikky and her friend Julie were at Manchester Airport to wave goodbye. I was talking to them when Sir Alex walked past on the concourse. I introduced manager to daughter and he just said simply, 'You're better looking than your father. He looks like a bulldog chewing a wasp.'

Sir Alex wasn't quite as witty on a United trip to Istanbul when assistant Brian Kidd burst into his hotel room late at night dressed as an Arab in robes, brandishing a sword. Kiddo remembers the gaffer didn't see the funny side.

David Beckham wasn't smiling either when he got on the wrong side of the boss after making his big breakthrough along with the rest of the Class of 92. I remember being at Old Trafford when Becks arrived for training in a second-hand sports car with a private 'Bex' registration. Sir Alex went mad, ordering Becks to have it removed by the morning.

I got on well with Becks, too, who along with Gary and Phil Neville gave me great interviews. I drank with their dads, Ted and Neville, on many foreign trips, with a memorable Tuesday afternoon jugging lager in Barcelona bars.

David was a great lad. I lost count of the number of times he appeared at Manchester Airport for a trip abroad – minus a passport left at home. We laughed about that after it was rushed to the terminal by taxi.

Becks gave me a rollicking once for a story he wasn't happy about, though. It was the nicest, most polite telling off I ever had in my life. He was certainly a charmer, although I'm reliably informed that he wasn't Victoria's first choice of a future husband when she paid a surprise visit to Old Trafford.

Victoria appeared with Sporty Spice on the pitch at half-time, and after the match they were invited into the players' lounge. Posh immediately had her eyes on Giggsy and sneaked her mobile number to him as he chatted to team-mates. The story goes that he wasn't interested (not like him) so Posh turned her attention to Becks and the rest is history, as they say.

To be fair, they were all good lads from the Brucie to Beckham years, with me unashamedly taking credit for a genuine quip on the arrival of Ole Gunnar Solskjaer at The Cliff in 1996 following his £1.5m transfer from Norwegian club Molde. I was waiting in the car park when Ole was driven in, sat in the back of a limo, and I took one look and said, 'Christ, it's the baby-faced assassin.'

I've mentioned before about befriending some of the great United legends. Another was Paul Ince, who Sir Alex sold to Inter Milan for £7.5m in June 1995. Peter Fitton, David Walker and I were on the same plane taking Ince and his wife Claire to Milan to complete the signing. He wasn't happy and I remember walking down the plane steps alongside him and him muttering, 'What the **** am I doing here?'

Ince had fallen out with Sir Alex big style. They hadn't seen eye to eye towards the end of Ince's United career, with Fergie labelling him a 'bottler' and 'a big-time Charlie'. Sir Alex had decided he was history but Ince was reluctant to leave Old Trafford, where he'd won two Premier League titles, two FA Cups, the League Cup and European Cup Winners' Cup.

There was no way back, though. And Ince knew it. But he still wasn't a happy bunny being unveiled in front of the Milan media and TV crews on the top floor of the Pirelli building in the centre of Milan. Ince refused to raise a smile, and when asked at the end of the unveiling whether he had any words for his new adoring Italian public, he muttered, 'Arrivederci.'

Memorable days. And magnificent nights, with one historic evening I'll never forget as long as I live on this earth – 26 May 1999, to be precise. Bayern Munich versus Manchester United in the Camp Nou, Barcelona, for their Champions League Final showdown. It was a match that looked beyond the reach of United when Mario Basler scored and the Germans dominated the rest of the match.

I was on my mobile to the office in London just starting my match report with ten minutes remaining to play. I can remember dictating: 'There were millions of tears flowing down from Heaven on what would have been Sir Matt Busby's 90th birthday ...'

Oh, hold on. Three minutes of injury time and, God almighty, Teddy Sheringham equalises. And then Solskjaer scores that dramatic, great late finish.

'Hello copy,' I stuttered down the phone. 'I need to make a change. This was the night millions of tears of joy flowed down from Heaven on what would have been Sir Matt Busby's 90th birthday ...'

It seems like yesterday. The trip to the interview room, passing Bayern supporters sobbing uncontrollably into steins of lager in the corridors. More tears flowing. And going deep down into the bowels of the Camp Nou, with Sir

Alex appearing around a corner on a golf buggy, clutching the Champions League trophy, and ordering his driver, kitman Albert, to steer towards me and mow me down.

It was madness with a capital 'M', with interviews to complete and copy to be sent to London. No wonder I was sweating up and in desperate need of a cooling beer myself. But I had a job to do and in the mixed zone where players depart the dressing room to meet the press, I struck gold. I interviewed Teddy Sheringham and he told me at the end to ask Sir Alex how he inspired his players at half-time to that ecstatic triumph.

The following day we'd been invited to the team hotel and I asked Sir Alex exactly what he'd said to the boys.

He told me, 'At the end of this game, the European Cup will be only six feet away from you and you'll not be able to touch it if we lose. And for many of you that will be the closest you will ever get. Don't you dare come back in here without giving your all.'

Enough said.

CHAPTER 7

AS YOU'VE read, United, Fergie and the boys played a large part in my *Mirror* career. But there were other clubs where memories were made, including Blackburn Rovers and one Mr Kenny Dalglish. Blackburn had gained promotion to the new Premier League in 1992 – a year after being taken over by businessman Jack Walker, who installed King Kenny as manager. Great move.

Kenny, who had masterminded the iconic signing of Alan Shearer, was a tough nut to crack in terms of relationships. He didn't suffer fools gladly and was happy to turn questions back to the embarrassed journalist who asked them. But I and close journalistic pals John Richardson and Billy Thornton weathered every press conference storm and had a great relationship with Kenny over a couple of eventful, historic years.

Millionaire owner Walker was approachable, too, and would always try to help with enquiries about the club and future transfers. However, it was always more productive phoning Jack at his luxury Jersey home after 5pm when his early evening whiskey drinking would begin. After a few glasses of Jameson he'd spill the beans on every footballing subject on earth.

He was certainly a character. A great man. No owner deserved his success more when Blackburn won the Premier League in 1995, albeit that he jumped the gun before the title was secured on that Sunday in May. Four days earlier, Blackburn had played a midweek match at Ewood Park and Jack celebrated like never before at the final whistle. He thought the victory meant that his beloved Blackburn had won the league.

Jack sprung out of his director's seat with a huge smile on his face, raising both arms in celebration and adulation of his club being crowned the kings of England. Fellow directors were quick to remind him that he'd jumped a very big gun.

But the calming down of jubilant Jack came too late to prevent the pitchside photographers from snapping the celebration picture for the following morning's newspapers. That signalled possibly the greatest back-page headline of all time with *The Sun* declaring above the arms-raised owner: 'Premature Jack Elation'. Priceless.

On the following Sunday, Jack finally got his wonderful wish despite Blackburn losing at Kenny's old club Liverpool. They had still edged out rivals Manchester United to win the Premier League. It was a double triumph for King Kenny, who had raised a glass to beating a press team at Blackburn's training ground just 48 hours before lifting the title trophy at Anfield.

We in the media had challenged Kenny to a game of football for most of the season and we thought it would never happen until he announced it was on – on the Friday before travelling to Merseyside.

So after the press conference duties were out of the way, we all headed into the training ground dressing rooms to get our kits on. Unfortunately, we'd left the strip supply to one Dave Maddock, who had foolishly approached rivals United to borrow a full set. So you can imagine the looks I got from the assembled Blackburn team waiting on the pitch as I appeared in Peter Schmeichel's actual Manchester United goalkeeping top. If Kenny and the boys were ever fired up to embarrass the press boys, they certainly were now.

The team Kenny selected proved he was deadly determined to show us who was boss. Scotland international striker Kenny was up front, with his assistant Ray Harford just behind, alongside the likes of Asa Hartford, Tony Parkes and, in goal, Shay Given of Blackburn, Newcastle and Manchester City fame.

We put up a good fight against such footballing class and were unlucky to come out 16-0 losers, although I still take great credit for saving three one-on-ones from King Kenny. To this day, he reminds me of that 90 minutes of humiliation and always asks, 'Are your fingers still bent back?' Even in his autobiography *Kenny Dalglish: My Liverpool Home*, he signed it: 'To Steve, how are your hands?'

It was a privilege to have met him and even more so to have received a phone call after his Blackburn exit when his mental strength in management had been ludicrously questioned. Kenny asked whether I could get the good guys in the press together and meet him at his favourite restaurant in Southport, Casa Italia. There over pasta and endless wine he poured out his heart and put the record straight. That was the human, emotional side of King Kenny that few ever witnessed. He was tough on the outside, cutting with his tongue, but always the man with a huge heart.

I remember many years later when I was on holiday with Syl and our pals Alan and Sue Dean. It was the Algarve as usual with our regular June day trip to Vila Sol to watch the superstars of football at Sir Bobby Robson's golf classic. They were all there: Kenny, Alan Shearer, Sam Allardyce, Peter Schmeichel. Working hard on the course and playing hard in the bar after the golf was over and before the presentation, which announced how many millions Sir Bobby's classic had raised for charity.

I knew my mate Alan was a big Liverpool fan and he couldn't take his adoring eyes off Kenny. So I went over to the great man and asked whether he'd say hello to star-stricken Al. Kenny did more than that. He brought wife Marina to our table and stayed for around half an hour, chatting mostly to Big Al, who would never forget the day he drank with his idol.

Earlier on that glorious sunny Vila Sol day, I'd walked the course, avoiding bumping into Big Sam Allardyce after upsetting him with some story I'd done about him. I was seriously dodging Mr Schmeichel, too. He still hadn't forgiven me about a story in the April 1997 when he missed the first leg of United's Champions League semi-final against Borussia Dortmund through injury.

Peter Fitton and I had pulled him at Manchester Airport before flying to Germany. He'd agreed to preview the following night's match, so with tape recorders at the ready we did our business. Halfway through I asked Schmeichel just how good this United side of the 90s was. How would he rate them?

We weren't prepared for the answer. Without hesitation, the great Dane looked me straight in the eye and said that because of new technology, better fitness, diet and all the trappings of the modern game, his United side would beat the 1968 European Cup-winning team 10-0. I inwardly gasped. Peter looked at me astonished. Schmeichel was adamant but wanted us to stress that the modern-day technology behind the current team would be the reason for such a mind-boggling scoreline. With that he rejoined the squad and we boarded the plane, not revealing until we landed what the United keeper had told us. We finally let this giant cat out of the bag and the boys went berserk. Could we go with such a damning verdict? Yes we could.

We all phoned our offices with the news and every sports editor in the land was in headline heaven. So the stories were sent and printed – and the following morning the incredible content relayed to Sir Alex and the squad in their team hotel in Germany.

The place erupted. 'We'd beat the '68 side 10-0' was the headline, which hit home and angered Sir Bobby Charlton, who was in that European Cup-winning team along with legends such as George Best, and Brian Kidd, now a VIP with the current squad.

Every office had played down the Schmeichel reasoning about modern-day technology being the difference between the two great sides. The headline only told half the story but offices don't bother about that.

Bobby certainly did as he entered the dressing room in Dortmund, I'm told. He sat next to Schmeichel, demanding an explanation. What he got was an emotional apology before the giant keeper came looking for me after the match. He stormed into the mixed zone and furiously confronted me and Peter as we spluttered that what he said was on our tapes. He didn't give a damn and issued every threat under the sun. Peter and I retreated behind the rest of the reporting gang to evade any possible physical punishment and thought that was the end of the embarrassment.

However, when I boarded the plane on that Wednesday night, I was handed a free paper by cabin crew – the *Mirror* with the '10-0' headline splashed across the back page. No wonder I got another daggers look as I passed Fergie, Martin Edwards and the whole of the United squad all reading that damning back page. So thank God that a couple of months later, in the peaceful surroundings of the Algarve, I was able to hide from another war with Schmeichel.

It was safer to keep my distance. Not like a previous summer when I played golf alongside my journalist pal Andy Dunn as we took on Kenny and Alan Hansen at their Hillside club in Southport. I still can't forget how we journalists were hammered again by Kenny and co. – and how they spent endless energy searching for ages for lost balls in the rough. They could have bought the golf club never mind a packet of Titleist.

Yes, it was a sad, sad day when King Kenny left Blackburn to be replaced by his chum Ray Harford, who was a lovely giant of a man. Sadly, filling Kenny's shoes proved too much of a task and two years later Ray was replaced by Roy Hodgson.

The future England manager wasn't an instant hit – with the fans or the players. The squad he inherited weren't happy that he made radical changes to their rest room and restaurant at the Brockhall training ground. Out went the pool tables, dartboards and card tables. In came wing-back armchairs, chessboards and draught sets, with players not encouraged to watch horse racing on the TV.

I must admit I didn't get on that well with Roy. After the humorous regime of Kenny and Ray we entered a new Blackburn media world of total rigidity. You were having a laugh Roy. It wasn't comfortable interviewing him either. One time in his office my questioning was continually interrupted by his phone ringing and Roy always picking up. He'd answer in Italian, French, Spanish. Stop the calls coming in, I thought. If he was trying to impress me by being multilingual it didn't work.

Blackburn wasn't the same place without Kenny and the boys. Nor when Kenny's title-winning striker Shearer left Ewood Park in July 1996 for a world-record-breaking transfer fee of £15m to join his hometown club Newcastle United. The Toon were managed by his hero Kevin Keegan and the news didn't get any bigger than Shearer going home with that kind of price tag around his head.

The *Mirror* immediately despatched me to the Far East to cover the huge story of Shearer joining his new team-mates on their pre-season tour. Newcastle were in Thailand and were to link up with the record signing in my birthplace, Singapore. The circle of life, as they say.

I flew from Manchester to Heathrow and linked up with fellow scribe and close pal John Richardson (Rico) for the 12-hour journey to Changi Airport, a flight that was ridiculously more sober and staid than the return trip was going to be. More of that later.

On arrival, we checked in at the team hotel and spied Shearer getting into the lift. John and I jumped in with him but he held up a protective hand and told us he wouldn't be doing any interviews. And he wouldn't be playing in any of the matches either, in Singapore or later in Japan. Damn. What a wasted journey for us was our first thought, until arriving at Shearer's floor, where we couldn't help but notice a soldier outside his bedroom door. 'Shearer's Armed Guard' was the next morning's headline to herald a week-long list of great back-page-hitting stories.

The following night we attended a Newcastle friendly against Japanese club Grampus Eight, who were briefly managed by future Arsenal legend Arsène Wenger. He was at the Singapore stadium and we interviewed him later, where he revealed that he'd been asked to work for the English FA. Another exclusive.

In our off-duty moments, Rico and I could be found enjoying the sunshine on the hotel's top floor, where I explained to my mate how in the past I'd always attracted the attention of gay men. I revealed that one particular night in Manchester I'd been propositioned by a guy in a sauna of a city centre health club. No sooner had that incident been relayed than I went for a dip in the hotel pool above the Singapore skyline. Minutes later, a stranger jumped in beside me, winked and tried a version of his own breast stroke on my unsuspecting body. Rico laughed and said, 'I know what you mean now.'

Next morning, we flew on to Osaka in Japan, picking up another story that Shearer couldn't fly with his new team because his world record valuation meant he'd exceeded Newcastle's insurance cover. Then one of the team medics revealed in the arrivals hall that they were worried about the superstar squad's health because Japan had suffered thousands of deaths due to dodgy prawns. Kerching.

While the exclusive story-getting was serious work, the media pack had its much lighter moments, too. Like one night out in Osaka when we stumbled into a bar advertising karaoke. We ordered bottles of beers, nuts and crisps and settled back to enjoy the entertainment. I was aware of what appeared to be the owner walking around the room bowing to all her customers, hands clasped in traditional mode. A beautiful lady dressed in a scarlet Japanese kimono.

Yours truly, being the creep I am, immediately took to the stage and sang in my best voice, Chris de Burgh's classic of 'Lady in Red'. I was a hit, with the kimono lady smiling and thanking me. That signalled a race to the stage for the rest of Her Majesty's press to belt out other classics to bring the Japanese house down.

We had a great time but weren't prepared for the monetary shock at the end of the night. The bill duly arrived at our table and the total for the five of us was well over £200.

'You're joking,' was one of the milder reactions. We'd only had five rounds of beer and a couple of bowls of snacks. You're having a laugh. Oh no they weren't. Seemingly in Japan *you* pay the bar for the privilege of singing karaoke and our endless hits had bumped up the bill alarmingly. We informed the Lady in Red that we Brits weren't coughing up so many Japanese yen and would just settle up for the beer and nuts.

Mistake. The Lady in Red withdrew into her office and minutes later three huge men in black approached our table and told us in broken English we'd be broken Englishmen if we didn't pay for singing for our supper. The rip-off bill was paid and we left the bar with a harsh lesson learned.

Drinking, of course, was a prominent part of our everyday life in Japan on that trip – and later on the Jumbo Jet back to England in the business class section adjacent to Newcastle's first class. Rico and I met up with a few of the lads an hour into the flight and they decided to play a drinking game. We'd start with sake in honour of our Japanese hosts. And then an hour later we'd order a round of beer followed by wine, whisky, vodka and tonic and so on and on and on.

By the eighth hour I was, let's say, totally relaxed, with Rico long gone, well beaten by his Newcastle heroes. He'd retired to his seat and I joined him with a complimentary bottle of wine. As if I hadn't had enough. I poured a glass, fell asleep and woke up with a jolt, my arm knocking the bottle of Merlot all over sleeping Rico.

CHAPTER 7

The rest of the flight was uncomfortable in more ways than one. But that's what being on tour as a journalist was all about.

CHAPTER 8

THAT 1997 day in Vila Sol I enthused about is still fondly remembered by yours truly all these decades later. Golf has always held a huge place in my heart, especially with what happened in the subsequent years of me being the proudest dad on the planet at Anthony's quest to finally rub shoulders with the world's greatest players at the 2004 Open.

So you can imagine what an honour it was to be sent by the *Mirror* to Valderrama in southern Spain for the Ryder Cup of 1997. Superstar Seve Ballesteros captained the European team to a memorable victory on his home soil and gave me a golden opportunity to report on one of the greatest events in sporting history.

To say it was an eventful week was a huge understatement. From beginning to end, I was fortunate enough to savour life, remembering experiences that are as vivid in my brain as they were all those pleasurable years ago.

It couldn't have got off to a better start, with the office telling me I'd be picked up at Malaga Airport by the *Mirror*'s London-based sports reporter Tony Stenson, who had caught an earlier flight.

I wasn't sure how we'd get on after knowing he wasn't too happy with my coverage of the 1994 World Cup in the USA from the desk under my stairs at Redwood Close. 'Stengun' was busy covering the competition Stateside but sports editor Dave Balmforth would send me a parcel of newspaper cuttings every day from newspapers worldwide. I'd write features and interviews to my heart's content and was plastered all over the *Mirror*, while Stengun only got a limited amount of space covering the World Cup in person. Oops.

Frosty was the word to describe our meeting in the airport parking lot, and the drive down the coast road to our apartment in San Pedro was quiet, to say the least. But it's amazing what a few drinks can do to break down barriers and build bridges. Although in Stengun's case it took a couple of bottles of Pinot Grigio in the bar at Valderrama. We soon became pals, a friendship that is strong to this day, and the laughs along the way will be etched in the memory for eternity.

That first night in our luxury abode was a memorable one. I woke up in the early hours to a huge swishing sound that I couldn't understand – until I popped my head around Stengun's bedroom door. There he was, mop and brush in hand, desperately sweeping away a torrent of water. He'd decided to leave his patio door open, unaware that a huge rainstorm was about to swamp the Costa del Sol beaches. Our apartment was in the storm's path and Stengun's room was quickly submerged under a foot of rain and sea water. Definitely more liquid than he'd downed a few hours before in the wine bar, which is saying something.

That was the start of the Ryder Cup mayhem as we discovered the following day that armed cops were patrolling the boundaries of Valderrama because of the threat of a terrorist attack. Hold the back page.

When play finally got underway on the Friday after a weather delay, I got another marvellous *Mirror* exclusive. I was following Ian Woosnam and he hit one shot to the right, straight into a packed army of supporters. They were of the Stars and Stripes variety and I was walking in front of the ropes to witness the first evidence of gamesmanship.

I watched in horror as two USA supporters stamped on Woosie's ball until it disappeared under the soggy ground. I pointed out the golfing crime, unaware that behind me had driven President George Bush Senior, alongside his wife Barbara in their USA buggy. President Bush asked me what had happened and I nervously explained the sequence of those disgraceful events. He was furious and immediately remonstrated with the apologetic Yanks before explaining what had occurred to the match officials. Woosie thanked Mr President for his concern. Got a free drop and made par. Game on.

I wasn't the only one to form a friendship with the president. My colleague Stengun bumped into him around the first tee – or was it the bar – and they immediately struck up a rapport. Stengun was sitting with another journalist when President Bush and the lovely Barbara wandered by and Bush said, 'Hi guys,' before shaking their hands. 'You're looking good, Mr President,' quipped the *Mirror* man to earn the reply: 'So are you.'

CHAPTER 8

Later in the day their paths crossed again further around
the course. Mr President spotted the wandering two and
said, 'Hi boys, how are you doing?' That, according to
Stengun, was the start of a lifelong friendship. Ermmmm.

I'd had another VIP moment the day before the Ryder
Cup started as I followed Lee Westwood around on his
final practice round. I was sat at the back of the sixth when
Lee played an approach shot, found the green and sank a
long putt for a birdie. Just as he departed for the next tee, I
turned to see Prince Andrew sitting under a tree, smiling,
shaking his head. I looked at him with a cautionary glance
as he said simply, 'That's some player. He's going to be a
great golfer in the future.' A simple statement of intent
that got me a back-page exclusive with the headline: 'Arise
Sir Lee'. Prince Andrew had given him the royal seal of
approval.

Other stories highlighted an amazing week, with
one particular American icon not taking the European
dominance with the grace and respect it deserved. Myself
and Stengun were enjoying yet another drink after work on
the Saturday night at one of the San Pedro bars. We looked
up to see Tiger Woods' caddy Fluff Cowan approaching.

'Hey Fluff,' we shouted. 'Come and have a drink with
the British press boys.' The look on his moustached face
told its own story. If looks could kill. With one rude gesture
of his arm, Fluff furiously declined our kind offer. That
proved just how much he hated the British press. Tiger
wasn't a fan either.

But in the end Europe had the last laugh and Seve
became the winning captain. It was a triumph tinged with

a tiny regret for the superstar Spaniard. He'd wanted to be the playing captain on home soil but there were concerns about a back problem and he wasn't allowed to swing a club in earnest.

The back was a touchy subject. One American journalist, who obviously had little knowledge of Seve or the Ryder Cup, asked if he could have a quick word with the golfing maestro. Unfortunately he referred to him as 'Steve' and not Seve, to which a furious Spaniard snarled, 'My name is Seve.' Lesson learned by the journalist, you might have thought. But oh no. He embarrassingly carried on with his questioning, asking for a quiet word but again referring to the golfing legend as 'Steve'.

Ballesteros understandably lost his temper and replied with a snarl, 'My name is Seve. Your name is arsehole.' Not bad viewing for those back in the USA.

Seve, yes Seve, guided Europe to an epic triumph and I'll always remember the final press conference before we said our goodbyes to Valderrama. The winning captain assembled all his triumphant team on the top table in the media room and one by one the players revealed their feelings on beating the USA and making Ryder Cup history.

I'll never forget that Woosie was last to get the mic and spent the intervening time drinking copious amounts of lager, wine, you name it. So by the time the cameras zoomed in on the loveable Welshman he was fast asleep, head bowed and snoring. Brilliant. Good job he'd been fully alert in gaining his valuable point for Europe.

I was reluctant to leave Sotogrande and head back to Malaga Airport with my driver Stengun. I'd had a wonderful time and was privileged to meet so many legends of the game of golf – and of course Mr President. But rubbing shoulders with the good and the great was always one of the perks of working as a national newspaper journalist.

I remember the *Mirror* signing up George Best to give his verdict on a Manchester United Champions League tie against Juventus at Old Trafford with a £2,000 fee happily agreed. To seal the deal, I was asked to meet the brilliant Bestie in the Midland Hotel in Manchester on the day of the match and, on arrival, I got reception to call his room. George's wife Alex came down and asked whether I could order a bottle of champagne to greet her hubby on his arrival – an hour later.

But I didn't care. I was delighted to pour the 'shampoo' into our three glasses as he asked me what the job entailed. I explained I'd call back at the Midland the following day before George and Alex caught the train back to Euston. All I wanted, I told him, was his view of United's performance against the Italians and the chances of winning the Champions League – a feat they completed two years later on that never-to-be-forgotten Camp Nou night.

George agreed. We polished off the champagne and I shook hands and left the bar, looking forward to what he had to say the next day.

United won after a memorable performance and I had a notebook full of questions to ask the great man. Again it took an age to drag Bestie down from his hotel room, with Alex once more appearing first and asking whether I could order the obligatory bottle of champagne. Of course. No problem. All on expenses anyway.

George finally appeared in our usual haunt of the bar and said we'd have to be quick because they had a train to catch in an hour. 'Right,' I said, ready to ask the obvious first question. 'What did you think of United's performance last night, George?'

The reply shocked me. 'No idea,' he said. 'Some of the old boys met me in the Midland last night and we went out for a good night on the town. Never saw one ball kicked.'

I told George that the sports editor had sanctioned two grand for his exclusive verdict, to which he replied, 'No problem. Write what you think and I'll be happy to go along with anything you say.'

So I did – after ordering another Moët for George, who never caught that lunchtime train back to London.

Money, though, was no object to the *Mirror* in those late 90s as they went for the big exclusives to gain vital circulation in the battle to compete with *The Sun*.

The sports desk sanctioned another hefty fee to sign up Les Ferdinand, who had joined Newcastle from QPR for £6m in 1995. I drove up to Newcastle's training ground and walked into the media room as arranged to link up with manager Kevin Keegan as a matter of courtesy. He greeted me with a handshake – and I didn't mention that blocking of my position in the school team all those years ago.

Then came a moment that summed up Kev's view of life. He spotted Andy Cole slowly making an exit via the back door with those loyal Toon supporters thronged at the front asking for autographs – and getting them from the whole squad. Cole had been having treatment upstairs and didn't think he had to scribble his name while he wasn't training. Think again, Coley.

Kev stopped him in his tracks with the question: 'Where you going? Get back out the front and sign every autograph you can for those kids whose dads pay your bloody wages. And don't come back in here for at least an hour.' Coley, head down, trooped out through the throngs to obey his manager's order. His quick, sneaky getaway totally scuppered. With that directive accomplished, Kev turned back to me with a huge smile on his face before pointing me in the direction of a side office where Ferdinand was waiting.

I must say Ferdy, as he is to this day, was brilliant in relaying the story of his life. He took me back to his early days at non-league Hayes and revealed exclusively how he nearly died one day going to training. He was in a car with team-mates, one of whom was driving too fast through a town on the way to the training ground. The driver misjudged a bend after flying over a hump-backed bridge and they crashed through a shop window, totally wrecking the car. Ferdy said he feared for his life but escaped with severe cuts and bruises. I wasn't going to revel in his near-death experience, but boy, what a great story it made for the *Mirror*.

I wrote a massive piece, complete with a hard news story for the back, but, incredibly, the story never saw the light of day. The sports department wanted to save it for a rainy day, which never came. So another few grand wasted by a poor decision in the office. There were a few of them on the *Mirror* but more of that later.

I just shrugged my shoulders and continued professionally with my job of covering the big teams such as Newcastle and Manchester United, the latter building up to that terrific 1999 treble of the Champions League, Premier League and FA Cup.

At this point I must mention another memorable moment with Becks, who was honoured by the Football Writers' Association at a lavish dinner at the Royal Lancaster Hotel in London. I was there that night with Syl, and after the meal guests queued to ask for Becks' autograph. I dragged Syl up with me to the top table, and although a couple of heavies tried to block my path to the United superstar, Becks beckoned me through. I turned back to grab Syl so I could introduce her but she refused to advance. She was far too starstruck to speak to the United and England great.

It was another glittering occasion I experienced, but the good times were about to come to a sudden, dramatic end to my star-studded career on the *Mirror*.

The writing started appearing on the wall when Des Kelly replaced Dave Balmforth as sports editor towards the end of those memorable 90s. I remember the first Sunday he was in the office and he phoned me at home in Redwood Close. He explained how delighted he was to be able to work with me after we'd formed a much earlier friendship at a Ryder Cup at the Belfry. But that respect quickly died in the coming months when we clearly didn't see eye to eye. I recall one brush with him and that other tool, editor Piers Morgan, in 1999.

United famously pulled out of the FA Cup after the FA told them of the possible risks to England's hopes of staging the next World Cup if they didn't take part in FIFA's new tournament, the World Club Championship, in Brazil. To explain their unprecedented decision, United held a press conference at Old Trafford to reiterate that their hands were clearly tied. Chairman Martin Edwards had also pulled me to one side to underline that it wasn't United's choice and they were acting in the best interests of the FA and a possible World Cup return to these shores after a ridiculous 34-year absence.

Before I could speak a word to the desk, Kelly phoned to say that madcap Morgan had ordered that the *Mirror* put the boot heavily into United for binning the FA Cup and I had to write an anti-United story. I refused point-blank and told Kelly that if Morgan wanted the story slanted that way then he could bloody write it himself. I'd seriously had my card marked by the club already and wasn't prepared to pen a bullshit version of heartrending events.

The irony wasn't lost on me that Morgan, a lifelong Arsenal fan, had an ulterior motive and an obvious hatred for the great team up north.

Basically, my career went downhill from there. I was attached to the *Mirror* office at Chadderton near Oldham and went there daily to write up stories and press conferences. And it wasn't long before I got to see messages from Kelly on my screen above stories I'd written that day. Some ordered his executives to 'get Millar to rewrite this shite. It's old news.'

I was livid. I've always accepted criticism but this was out of order. Unfair. And totally unacceptable to inform the whole office in Canary Wharf that I was crap at doing what I'd done best in my whole successful career. I was left with no alternative but to phone Kelly and put the record straight. Why was he being so critical when I could write him under the table?

He accepted the call and ordered me to the London office on the Monday. I stopped him in his tracks. 'Sorry,' I informed him, 'can't do that. My son is in Scotland trying to qualify for the Open and he's much more important to me than you are, pal.' With that, Kelly reluctantly rescheduled for later in the week and I made the journey down to Canary Wharf to be met with unexpected hostility.

I maintained my patience when he kept me waiting for almost two hours and eventually he beckoned me into his office high in the Canary Wharf skyline. I was stunned by what he did next. Kelly had endless piles of my stories with phrases that he detested underlined in yellow. Time after time he repeated what he hated in my story context. Then he announced that one of his assistants, Dominic Hart, had taped my conversations with the sports desk and they thought my language was deplorable.

I was now furious. How dare Hart, who I'd never met, record what I'd said when describing what stories I'd be sending. Christ, we were working on a newspaper not in a convent. Swearing was rife in the workplace. And anyway, wasn't it illegal to tape what I'd said? Bang out of order.

To add insult to injury, Kelly informed me that he was appointing this numbskull Hart as my senior executive. Every morning I was to report to him about what stories I'd be working on and he'd tell me how to write them.

Get real. A no-hoper like Hart – who ludicrously went on to become sports editor – being my sole adviser? Kelly could think again.

I walked out of his office in a temper and passed by his man Hart on the way to the lift, threatening to throw him out of the window on the 34th floor for doing me in. My head was spinning with what Kelly had said and what Hart had done. I'd never been treated like that in my life.

I found my way to the Dockland Railway platform in a haze, boarded the train, and once on the track, glanced back at the fast disappearing Canary Wharf tower block. I knew at that emotional moment I'd never go back there again.

CHAPTER 9

I WAS deep in thought all the way to Euston and again on the train journey to Milton Keynes, where I'd left my car. What the hell would I do? I couldn't operate under those ludicrous conditions. To run my story past one of Kelly's sidekicks and he'd guide me on how to write it? No chance. That hopeless Hart telling me how to do my job? Get a life.

And that's what I needed now. A new life. But first I had to talk it over with a journalist I respected so much, Peter Fitton of *The Sun*. He'd asked me to give him a ring after meeting Kelly and I just had enough power left in the office mobile to call Peter as soon as I reached my car. He was sympathetic and then as angry as me. With that, he advised me on my next move – to go to my doctor the next morning and speak to him about being signed off work on medical grounds.

I remember going to the surgery with Syl and breaking down uncontrollably as I told the doctor of my appalling predicament of basically being bullied in the workplace. He was so understanding and didn't hesitate in giving me a sick note for an initial fortnight – and would sign me off for as long as I wanted. I desperately needed to get my head straight and sleep at night.

I wasn't that bad a journalist was I? After all my years of experience, did I suddenly need someone to tell me how to write a story? Was I the hopeless case who had risen to deputy sports editor on the *Sunday Mirror*, became sports editor of the *Daily Sport* and who had been offered the sports editor's job on *The People*?

Those morons in Canary Wharf clearly thought I was a bad journalist. I knew I bloody wasn't but would never win the battle against Kelly and no-hoper no-Hart. And certainly there would be no support from *Mirror* editor Piers Morgan, who had seriously ignored me on that last trip to Canary Wharf.

I sat down with Syl – in the pub naturally, the Rope and Anchor at Woolston – and we candidly discussed the future. I opened up that the job on the *Mirror* was ripping me apart. I actually feared for my life with what I thought was a heart attack on the near horizon.

I told Syl that I felt trapped. Her reply will stay with me forever. She said, 'You should never feel trapped in your life. If you want to leave then let's leave and just do it. It's not worth making yourself so ill.'

The whole heavy world lifted off my sagging shoulders. Yes, the *Mirror* was no longer with the Millar.

Jobs on other newspapers were at a premium so I – and later Syl – came to the life-changing decision that I had to get away from the *Mirror* madmen. Get a life. Literally.

And then came the lightbulb moment. Something I'd always wanted to do. Probably from the early childhood days when I'd help my dad Stan bottle up in the Buffaloes Lodge bar at RAF Lindholme where he worked part-time. Run a pub.

But where? How? So what better man to ask for his advice than my great mate Alan Dean who still had strong contacts at Burtonwood Brewery outside Warrington, where he'd once climbed the promotion ladder. I put it to Al that I saw my future in the pub trade and he was quick to give me some solid advice, which went on the lines of: 'Don't be so bloody stupid, Steve.' No. No. A hundred times No. Al couldn't make it any clearer that quitting newspapers and getting a pub would be a huge mistake.

But I wouldn't take Al's emphatic 'no' for an answer and pleaded with him to help with an introduction to executives at Burtonwood. Thank God he did.

Al gave me Mark Cullen's phone number and I duly rang him, introducing myself as Al's buddy, which got me on the inside track at the brewery. Anyone Al was recommending was going to be the right guy for the job.

I duly met Mark and his boardroom colleagues and they revealed that they had just purchased the Antelope Inn at Congleton, Cheshire, for £250,000 and were looking for a landlord and landlady. Syl and I fitted the bill, I was hastily informed. Seemingly, they were having difficulty employing publicans who weren't adorned with tattoos and piercings. So after a very limited form of interview, Burtonwood said the Antelope was ours if we wanted to give it a go.

I couldn't wait to tell Al and his lovely wife Sue, and that first Friday night we ventured into Congleton to take a look at what was to become our home for three eventful, never-to-be-forgotten years. We walked up Lawton high street and peered through the lounge window of what was a magnificent black-and-white timbered building. It was around 8.30pm and the pub was packed. Drinkers four deep at the bar.

I looked at Al. He at me. This was a great, hopefully money-spinning sight to behold. And we both agreed, along with the girls, that running the Antelope would hopefully be a lucrative move. A haven for me, at least, away from the *Mirror* morons. I knew at that moment, when I first stepped into the pub, that this was where I wanted to be.

But it wasn't as easy as that. First and foremost I had to ensure that Syl was in total agreement, which, thankfully, she was. We both wanted Syl to keep her job in Warrington and commute, although that in itself presented later problems. Then we had to think, of course, of the kids. Nikky was 24, working at Expotel in Stockport, and Anthony, at 21, was carving out his golfing career. They were positive, thank goodness, about their dad's dramatic change of career, and the support from Syl, Nikky and Anthony was overwhelming and very much appreciated.

I couldn't wait to pick up the phone to ring Burtonwood and give them a positive 'yes'. We'd love to take over at the Antelope. But first I had to enrol at the brewery for a hurried course on pub management, understand the licensing laws – and pass the licence examination. That tough task was answered in three days and I could officially put my name above the Antelope door as a bona fide pub landlord.

We were all set for the next Millar adventure, with Anthony continuing to live at 3 Redwood Close until I made the stupid decision to sell our beautiful four-bedroomed house for a ludicrous £108,000 in October 1999 – a month after moving into the Antelope. Why the hell didn't I put the house on the lettings market instead of rushing into a quick sale? I regret that decision to this day. Bloody stupid me. Regrets, I've certainly had a few. And that was right up there with the biggest.

But let's move on. Basically, Anthony had nowhere to live so he packed his bags for the pub in that October and became an Antelope resident in the bedroom just down the corridor from his sister's boudoir. One happy family with a lovely roof over our heads – and wonderful memories to be cherished to this day.

Our Antelope doors were opened on Wednesday, 15 September 1999 at 7pm to signal three years of fun, frolics and friendships that you could write a book about.

Well, I just have.

CHAPTER 10

I'M WRITING this chapter on the Millars' pub adventure on my 69th birthday – a milestone I never thought I'd reach in my colourful, eventful life. As I've said, my late teenage years were full of heartbreak, with first my granddad Jack dying, followed 12 months later by the horrendous death of my dad Stan. Then my lovely grandma Kitty passed, and my auntie Rita, uncles Peter and Harry also ascended to Heaven. My mum was later taken, too, and Syl's mum and dad Lily and Harry.

So much sadness to suffer in those 69 years, where you learn to savour every moment on this sometimes difficult and emotional journey through the ages. To count your blessings for the wonderful family you have in your life and cherish the new generation growing up, hopefully for many years ahead. To be proud of the dynasty Syl and I have created between us. To embrace physically and mentally our two children, Nikky and Anthony, their special spouses Andy and Clare, and six beautiful grandchildren, George, Daisy, Molly, William, Sophie and one more Harry.

I know they would have loved, as we did, those 36 months Syl and I spent in Congleton, where new friendships were forged to last a lifetime. We fell in love with that little Cheshire town where legend tells that in the 1620s the locals saved to buy a bible but the money was spent instead on purchasing a bear. Hence the nickname 'Beartown'.

Our new home, of course, became the Antelope, with Syl seriously mithered that first Wednesday, handling the financial side of the handover. I was sweating on my final licensing examination back at the Burtonwood base while Syl was busy writing cheques, including the big one for the fixtures and fittings, a cool £16,000. We agreed on a £12,000-a-year rent, and the formalities, it seemed, were complete.

The only trouble was that the Antelope's owners for the last 26 years, John and Anne, weren't in any hurry to vacate the premises. In fact, John made it clear he was going nowhere. He stayed in his bedroom, refusing to come down the stairs and exit the front door on to Lawton Street to start their new retired life up the road just outside Congleton. John was distraught and stayed locked in his room for a good few hours before Syl saw the sad sight of him being led down the stairs and out of the door for the final time in his life.

Syl waved goodbye, too, to the Burtonwood executives and was flustered to say the least when I eventually showed up with a big smile – and, more to the point, my liquor licence. My name went above the entrance and we busily prepared for the opening night. The beer lines were all connected, cash was in the till that we didn't know how to use and we counted down the clock to the first through the door at the big 7pm opening.

That turned out to be Malcolm and his near neighbour Ted, whose trademark departure over the subsequent years when finishing his final pint was always the same: 'Well, as they say in Russia, I Moscow.' Both were given free beer for being our first customers and everyone else that momentous night was given a handshake and introduction from the Antelope's new and very nervous hosts.

There were mistakes made, of course. Calculating how much change to have for the till was a minefield and I can still see Syl and Sue pounding the streets of Congleton begging chemists and other pubs for pound coins. I still don't know to this day how I changed barrels so confidently or cleaned my beer lines so skilfully every Wednesday to keep the customers – and Sir Alex – happy. The Manchester United manager's advice on running a pub was etched in my brain and I got a full-page write-up in the local *Congleton Chronicle* for my sports writing career, accompanied by photographs of me with Fergie and Brazilian superstar Pelé.

I'd revealed in the article that Sir Alex had promised he'd call in to the Antelope on the way to Stoke, although, sadly, he never did. But other footballers, including former Manchester City stars Ian and David Brightwell, were regular customers along with their famous mum and dad Ann and Robbie, who starred in the 1964 Olympic Games in Tokyo.

On a more mundane sporting level, I was quick to ask my new clientele whether there was a local football team and

I was reliably informed that there was, Congleton Athletic, who played in the Cheshire League. I further enquired where they went to eat after matches and was pointed in the direction of another local hostelry. Seemingly, though, the boys weren't happy that they were being charged for their burger and chips.

'Tell them that they can dine at the Antelope for nothing,' I announced in another lightbulb moment. Word spread quickly and I was soon pouring pints for goalkeeper Tonks, pals Phil and Chris, and Athletic manager Kev (more of him later on). We shook hands on getting the boys back to my pub on a Saturday afternoon, where they could scoff on the house to their hearts' content.

I also persuaded Burtonwood Brewery to supply a sponsored kit, and for three cup finals I put on a players' coach stocked with hefty supplies of canned lager. The boys were delighted and they became regulars at the Antelope on a Saturday night, bringing along with them their wives or girlfriends to bulge the tills with cash.

Me and Syl were having a ball, too, with not only a captive audience in the footy boys but also a new group of locals who packed the pub on Friday and Saturday nights. We had fun and frolics galore. Laughed loads. Memories for eternity. The atmosphere inside the Antelope was electric with my tainted life on the *Mirror* a thing of the past.

But while the Antelope was buzzing, we had a couple of incidents that emphasised just how difficult life as a landlord could be. The first was on our debut Sunday opening when in the early afternoon the front door swung open for the appearance of one notorious individual. Maggot was his name and he headed a line of heavy-looking guys and their glamorous molls. The pub fell silent. You could almost see the tumbleweed following the gang from Mow Cop, a village high up on the Cheshire-Staffordshire border with a widely reported reputation for inter-breeding.

My new regulars looked straight at me as Maggot and his followers exited for the beer garden. Everyone warned me that I didn't want them in the Antelope. I was spooked but immediately approached them while they were sitting on benches without having ordered any drinks. I held my hand out to the man called Maggot, introduced myself and told him that I wouldn't tolerate any drug-taking or threatening behaviour. With that, he stood up, nodded to the rest of the gang and they departed the pub, never to be seen on the premises again. Phew.

I also had a next-door neighbour called Sharon who was weird to say the least. She'd appear for no apparent reason at the front window just staring at me behind the bar, wearing just her nightclothes. Talk about a psycho on your doorstep. She christened me Kenny Rogers, after the country singer, because of my beard, and would sometimes just appear in the pub with a puppy stuffed under her nightdress. I was quick to get rid of scary Sharon.

There was also a visit after around 12 months from a six-foot something who had just been released from Strangeways in Manchester. He strode up to the bar one night, looked me in the eye and then at the ceiling and chillingly announced that up there was where he blasted a shotgun above the head of another landlord in the town.

I bravely refused him a drink and he left with a threat reverberating in my ears.

What do I do? Call the police? Inform them of the threat? What? Then I had a brainwave. I discovered his girlfriend had a dog-grooming business, so I phoned to book in our golden cocker spaniel Harriet. I put on the charm offensive and found out later that she'd informed him that Steve and Sylvia were so lovely. She must have read the riot act because we never saw him again until our final week, when he came up to the bar and admitted that he'd never called in since his silly threat because he didn't want to scare the customers.

Another escape from potential harm, with only one incident to report in our three years at the Antelope. That came a couple of months into our new life, again on a Sunday, with a wedding party enjoying a drink the day after the marital vows. One guy called Jack was sitting on a stool at the bar when he had a few cross words with another local called 'Big and Daft', who furiously left the pub, shaking his head in rage. I thought no more of it until 'Big and Daft' suddenly reappeared brandishing what I thought was a sword. Christ almighty. A bloody samurai warrior in sleepy Congleton.

It turned out to be a stool leg he'd broken off when returning to his flat and Jack got the full weight of it on the back of his head. There was a furious scuffle. Punches were thrown before 'Big and Daft' departed, leaving Jack prone on the floor nursing a serious head wound. Police and ambulance crew were called, with bloodied Jack lucky to escape a hospital visit. 'Big and Daft' was, naturally, handed a ban that would remain until we departed the Antelope.

That emotional exit to return to Warrington came in September 2002, when I learned a lot more about Congleton Athletic manager Kev. I'd spent those three previous years poking fun at Kev, brandishing him a Clark Kent lookalike. Bit of a geek really. Then our goalkeeper Tonks sidled up to me at one of our two farewell parties and informed me that Clark Kent Kev was the head slaughterman at a Stoke abattoir.

'You know you've taken the mickey out of Kev for all these years? Well, just to let you know, he's the hardest man in the Potteries, and when you and Sylvia arrived at the Antelope he sent out a warning to any potential troublemakers. He declared that if anyone hurt or worried Sylvia and Steve, then they would answer to him.'

Thanks to this day Kev, you lovely man. More Superman than Clark Kent.

So, as you can see, we had a few dodgy moments. But they in no way clouded our judgement that life at the Antelope was a real game-changer. A tumultuous time when Westlife and Boyzone were the backdrop to our loving catalogue of momentous memories.

CHAPTER 11

JOURNALISM WAS never far from my thoughts as I adjusted to my new life behind the bar and down in the cellar. In fact, I reported on a Saturday for the *Mail on Sunday*, mainly covering Stoke, Port Vale and Crewe, and collecting a welcome £140 in the process. But travelling to matches the day after the night before sometimes proved a little bit precarious if confronted by a member of Her Majesty's constabulary.

One such moment came on a Saturday lunchtime when I was making my way through Alderley Edge en route to the Reebok Stadium to cover a Bolton match. I'd had a late, late but great lock-in on the Friday night, with the last customers leaving the Antelope at about 1am. Then Syl and I retired to our lovely rooftop terrace, where generous amounts of wine were consumed to round off another successful night in the boozer below.

So the next day it was a heart-stopping moment when I rounded a bend just before High Street to be confronted by a bobby ordering me to pull over. He at first gave me a ticking-off because his speed gun registered that I was travelling a few miles over the 30mph limit. Then he stepped nearer to ask whether I'd been drinking. I informed him I was running a pub and had been in the cellar that morning so it was natural that alcohol would be in the air around me.

That didn't fool this policeman, who immediately reached for his breathalyser and asked me to blow hard. Before I did, I muttered that it was his lucky day as I'd had a skinful and was very late to my bed. But astonishingly – and much to his utter disgust – my breath test wasn't as positive as he'd have liked and with a shake of the head he told me to get off his patch. I felt like having a drink to celebrate that lucky escape. It still amazes me to this day that after all those endless hours of necking Strongbow and red wine my boozy breath didn't go off the Richter scale in his breathalyser kit.

That rooftop terrace, though, was our late-night and early-morning sanctuary. Our pride and joy. A private place surrounded by garden centre plants and bushes for privacy, with two reclining chairs for comfort while we drank.

I don't think Big Al took our extra supplies under the stars into his figures for the three-monthly stocktake. He was convinced we were being ripped off by one of the bar staff but we were just basically helping ourselves to the wine stock and keeping mum. He was, though, pretty impressed with our official figures each week, with regular increased takings of around £6,000.

We had great staff, too, after eventually finding our chef in the shape of army-trained Jo, who came to our rescue after we got rid of around five unworthy predecessors. Our bar manager, too, was a big plus in the little shape of Char. When we interviewed her for a job behind the bar she was so nervous she broke down in tears when Syl began talking to her about the role. She may have been petite but she grew into the job with giant confidence and didn't take any nonsense from customers trying it on or being a nuisance.

Nikky and Anthony worked the bar, too, along with some of our daughter's Warrington mates who gladly made the journey that Syl hated to bring in a whole bunch of new, admiring customers. I must admit I did push the boundaries a bit, especially when I got these gorgeous young girls to dress up in bunny outfits behind the bar at Easter, including Nikky of course. Sorry girls. But you were a real attraction to get drooling guys through the doors of the Antelope and further boost the till takings.

They also got the sleepy town buzzing again at our one-and-only participation at the Congleton Carnival, where one of the local lads provided a lorry from his company to join the parade. We bought bales of hay to scatter on the low-loader and built a bar so the scene resembled a Wild West saloon. Nikky and her mates became can-can dancers dressed in colourful Moulin Rouge corsets and costumes and high-kicked their way around Congleton's roads on the back of the lorry. The more high-kicks they performed, the more smiling carnival-goers lining the Congy streets threw their notes and coins on to the 'saloon' floor.

Once the parade reached the town hall, Nikky and her can-can pals were in full flow, much to the further delight of the VIP guests seated in a stand outside the entrance. This included the MP for Macclesfield, Nicholas

Winterton, who couldn't take his eyes off the Antelope dazzlers and threw loads of cash at the girls' feet – much to the annoyance of his Congleton MP wife, Ann.

But as well as having attractive bar staff on a Friday and Saturday night, we got the town buzzing again with our monthly karaoke nights. My old golfing mate Andy Wright travelled over from Warrington every month to set up the decks and mics and fill the pub with great singers. None more so than Andy himself.

Our occasional nights off were something to sing about, too. We got tax relief of £30 a week to visit rival hostelries and restaurants in Congleton, with Reuben Stubbs just down High Street our favourite.

There was another little perk that made us smile, too. There was another fiver a week to pocket for classing our golden cocker Harriett as a guard dog. Burglars must have been shaking in their shoes – not.

Not that we were ever raided, although one Christmas really brassed us off. We'd laid on free nibbles and drinks for Christmas lunch and, as you would expect, we had a packed pub of revellers. But unknown to us, a family who had rarely visited the Antelope were raiding our outside freezers and chucking food over the beer garden wall to other relatives to flee with a lovely Christmas feast.

That, though, was a rare event when we felt betrayed trying to make a living in my new trade and profession in our new Congleton home. That unsavoury incident shouldn't taint – and hasn't tainted – what was an incredible three years in a town of honest-to-goodness folk who will be remembered so fondly by the whole Millar family for all time.

So when the last orders bell rang for that final time in September 2002, it was with a heavy heart that we said farewell to our new friends and headed back to Warrington with a misguided thought that I could retire. We were led to believe by our financial 'experts' that my *Mirror* pension was bursting the bank vault doors and we both thought of heading off to pastures new in Spain after viewing many, many properties.

But financial reality brought us back down to earth and we chose instead to remain on home shores with a six-month rental in Mitchell Street, Stockton Heath, our next move. It was a cramped terrace house to say the least, with ceilings low enough for me to continually repeat the old joke that the place was so small even the mice had hunched backs.

We were happy in Mitchell Street, though, and it was in the London Bridge pub at the end of our street that Nikky introduced us to her new boyfriend, Andy, who shuffled over on crutches, having broken his leg playing football. They, of course, would marry later, but all that was in the future.

The present was six months for me looking out of the window every dull day and wondering what I'd do with my life now I had no job and couldn't afford a luxurious retirement on the Costas. A phone call from my old mate on the *People*, sports editor John Maddock, provided Millarman with the next chapter in this book and in my journalistic career.

CHAPTER 12

THE OUT-OF-THE-BLUE call from John was the start of a magical new part of our lives. From feeling down, I was definitely on the up when Express Newspapers' new managing director explained the exciting new venture within the group. The plan was to launch a new newspaper, the *Daily Star Sunday*, from the *Lancashire Evening Post*'s printing plant on the outskirts of Preston. And John was on the phone asking whether I fancied the idea of joining him, sports editor Ray Ansbro and the rest of the editorial staff as an adviser.

Well, obviously I'd been there before at the start of another new newspaper and I didn't hesitate. The next day I was in the office putting up ideas and before I knew it John asked whether I'd accept his offer of a three-day-a-week job on the sports writing side.

Yes couldn't come out of my mouth quickly enough and that was the start of a 16-year journey covering every Open golf championship, two Ryder Cups, 15 Grand Nationals and at least a dozen Wimbledons. In addition, there were adventures abroad alongside my new colleague,

Paul Hetherington, who had originally recommended me for the job.

Oh, and Syl and I had just bought a house, too, paying £119,950 for our lovely terrace abode in East View, Grappenhall, in March 2003. My life was back on track. In work again and living in a wonderful area on the south side of Warrington where we're still residing as I recollect the journey into eventual retirement.

Football again became my main concern, and a reunion with Sir Alex at United's Carrington training complex, where another whack on the back of my head as he entered the conference room told me he was glad to see me back in business.

I was definitely on a high and quickly settled into my new three-day role with a Premier League match on a Saturday finishing every eventful week. But that high-rocketed to the stars the following year when son Anthony amazingly qualified for the 2004 Open at Royal Troon. My God, I can still feel the adrenaline rush – and shiver at the drama of it all – as he was successful in the final qualifier at Glasgow Gailes after getting through pre-qualifying at Little Aston golf club in the Midlands.

Those two days on the Glasgow track will live with me forever. We'd always supported Anthony in previous qualifiers, with shredded nerves always getting the better of me. I remember one early tournament where I was so, so nervous on the first tee that I crawled under a car to watch him drive off through shaking fingers.

Now, we were back to business in Glasgow Gailes with Anthony in great form and finally going head to head with another young golfing hopeful for the final place at Troon in a dramatic play-off.

Nikky was about to give birth to baby George and stayed in the clubhouse with Syl while I and Nikky's husband-to-be Andy followed Anthony down the first play-off hole. All square was the result after Anthony sank a ten-foot putt to level with a par.

Then it was on to the next hole, a tricky elevated par three with Ant's opponent hitting left and off the green. Anthony kept his cool to fire on to the green and win the hole – and his precious place at Royal Troon.

What a magical moment to experience and savour. My heart pounded. Pride exploded through my body as I wanted to run and hug my boy but hesitated. The sight of his opponent, head down and seriously upset, meant I delayed the celebrations out of respect for a great young golfer in defeat. However, I couldn't hold it in later, as I filled up the car at a petrol station for the journey home, screaming, 'My son's in the Open!'

As the Millars headed back to Grappenhall, Anthony and bride-to-be Clare were whisked into another world by Ant's golfing sponsor Wilson, who found them top-class accommodation. The next thing is that my boy was catapulted into stardom, with my golfing pal Tony Stenson calling to say Anthony had been unveiled at Troon on the same table as Padraig Harrington on the Monday of the Open week to endorse Wilson products in a news conference.

And it only got better. I shot back to the famous links on the Wednesday, where Anthony was playing his final practice round. What happened next still amazes me to this day. Anthony was waiting on the tee a few holes from home when suddenly Canadian Mike Weir approached and asked whether he could play in with him. Jesus, the Masters champion of 2003 wanting to partner my son.

And he did. What a guy. What a hero. What a source of inspiration when he took Anthony to one side after they had walked off the 18th. I was intrigued and immediately quizzed Anthony on his return, his face creased with a smile almost as wide as the Royal Troon fairways.

'What did he say?' I asked, to which Anthony replied, 'He said whether you make the cut or not, remember that when you are on the first tee tomorrow you are one of the best 156 golfers in the world.'

Wow. That was some statement from the 17-time winner on the PGA and European tours. No wonder Anthony was walking ten-feet tall as he got ready for the opening day, teeing off in the last group at almost 4.30 pm.

Anthony made a great start and was level par until misfortune plagued his round, although I'll remember forever his recovery on the eighth, escaping the notorious Coffin bunker with a wonderful shot. The cheers were so loud that an American raced away from the stand-side refreshment wagon to ask clapping fans, 'Was that Tiger on the green?'

Sadly, Anthony did miss the cut but that will never darken the brightest of two days when our son walked on the same fairways as the greatest golfers in the world. It would be impossible to match those memorable two rounds at Royal Troon for heart-bursting pride, excitement and sheer joy of watching my son make his own golfing history.

I still recall with a smile Anthony being disappointed that Tiger Woods walked past him going to the practice ground without releasing a nod or a smile. And I can chuckle too at the sight of Anthony following the great Nick Faldo to the PGA marquee where golf fans chucked caps over the fencing into the VIP walkway in the hope of getting them signed. Faldo walked straight ahead, ignoring the autograph pleas, until Anthony stopped him in his tracks and held out a couple of caps saying, 'You need to sign these, Nick.' He duly did.

And while my heart was heavy at Anthony's departure on the Friday evening, nothing can ever mask that Mike Weir statement that Anthony for those two days was one of the best 156 golfers in the world.

What was difficult for this doting dad was trying to unscramble my brain and get back to the job of covering the 2004 Open for the *Daily Star Sunday*. And I admit that being asked by sports editor Ray Ansbro to write at length my account of Anthony's Open experience for our newspaper was a seriously emotional one. The words and the tears flowing in unison, remembering that my late dad Stan would surely have been looking down from Heaven's 19th hole, raising a glass to this latest Millar's heroics.

But life went on, as it does. And my experiences and adventures over the next 15 years will remain etched in the memory for all time.

I have vivid recollections of covering the 2006 World Cup in Germany and being there at the infamous Cristiano

Ronaldo 'winker-gate' when England played Portugal in Gelsenkirchen. Ronaldo's Manchester United team-mate Wayne Rooney was red-carded for a second-half stamping incident with the Portuguese superstar caught on camera winking as Roo headed for the dressing room.

England were cursed by their regular penalty shoot-out failure after a scoreless draw and Paul and I wrote endless words on the incident that had angered the nation. We all expected Rooney to land one on Ronaldo's chiselled chin but seemingly the England superstar never gave his Old Trafford team-mate any stick. He bloody should have done.

The following year Paul and I were on our travels again, this time to Tel Aviv where England drew with Israel. We stayed in a beautiful hotel overlooking glorious sandy beaches and clear blue seas. Idyllic, you would have thought, until our beach bar waiter informed our journalistic drinking party that this was an area often heavily damaged by Palestinian rocket attacks. In fact, the bar we were in had been obliterated during one such heavy raid. Needless to say, we drank our drinks faster than you could say 'take cover'. We hurried away down a boardwalk with us all strangely singing the Proclaimers' famous words: 'I would walk 500 miles.'

I flew many, many more miles than that when I was sent to the 2010 World Cup in South Africa, where I stayed for just over three weeks to cover the tournament. I and *Sunday Express* colleague Jim Holden were based in Sandton, an exclusive banking centre based on the outskirts of Johannesburg. We were accommodated in a beautiful apartment block overlooking the city but still within earshot of those irritating vuvuzelas, which were blown 24 hours a day until South Africa were knocked out of the competition.

Two days after arriving we were off to the opening ceremony in the Soccer City stadium just the other side of Johannesburg, where we got our first dreaded proof that this wasn't a safe place. Our minibus driver, a former SAS-type South African soldier, pointed to a row of beautiful Portuguese-style villas on the journey to the stadium. Each wall surrounding their swimming pools and patios was lined with razor wire and he said it was his job to 'tidy up' at weekends when he'd be called out by the affluent residents. It was there on millionaires' row that he'd discovered the bodies of black people who had scaled the guarded walls trying to break in. The owners had shot them dead and it was the driver's role to collect the corpses and dump them in a place secret to him.

That was our first grim and stark reminder of the hostilities of black and white living apart and not together in apartheid-riddled South Africa. The driver spoke calmly and clearly about collecting bodies with no police interference and certainly no murder charges being brought.

But then again, black lives in that part of the world clearly didn't matter, with another warning given to us if we were going to hire a car to travel to matches. We were told by our security team that if we did and we drove through townships we'd need to be fully alert when pulling up at traffic lights. The trick to steal your car was for some guy to lie down in front of your wheels. If that happened, then just drive over him. It didn't matter, we were calmly informed.

It was clear that this was going to be some experience. But there were some lighter notes. Like the advice not to walk under trees because snakes could be hiding in the branches ready to glide down and attack. Oh, and even though this was July, no one had warned us how cold it could be. My second match in Johannesburg was a hellish night. I only had a shirt on. No jacket. And I was shivering like hell in the press box. At half-time, I sought warm refuge in the media centre and huddled my arms around a free-standing heater. One puzzled media assistant asked me whether I was okay and I explained my cold discomfort.

'What do you expect,' she coolly exclaimed. 'This is our winter and that's when snakes freeze solid in the fields.'

No surprise then that the next day I was quickly off to the Sandton shopping villages to buy a padded jacket to keep warm for the rest of the eventful time in South Africa. However, it wasn't as bleak in the beautiful city of Cape Town, where we stayed in a luxury hotel with breathtaking views of Table Mountain. That's some place.

I felt the cold two years later, though, in Oslo when England chalked up a 1-0 victory against Norway, their first win in 32 years over their opponents. The match wasn't very eventful but the night before certainly was. About eight of us journos had arranged to meet in the harbour area at a lovely restaurant, and one, dear old Bob Cass, had arrived ahead of the gang. When the rest of us finally showed up and got seated, Bob asked us whether we'd like to taste the wine he'd ordered. That's a bit presumptuous, I thought. How did he know what we all liked?

On leafing through the wine list we soon discovered that the *Mail on Sunday* man had ordered *eight* bottles of Cloudy Bay – at £80 a bloody bottle. I was livid with my old mate and refused to drink a drop before moving out to a restaurant next door, knowing I wouldn't be able to get that share of the wine bill past the tight *Daily Star Sunday* cashiers. We laughed about it later, with Cloudy Bay-gate a treasured memory when talking about the late, great Bob Cass.

CHAPTER 13

BACK HOME in dear old Blighty there were always plenty of memorable incidents as I continued covering football, golf, tennis and horse racing.

I was sent in recent years to cover the Scottish Open and remember one time asking Ian Poulter before a practice round whether I could sit him down for an interview. To my surprise he said, 'Don't hang around for five hours, let's do it now.'

I reminded Poults that he was about to go to the first tee and there wasn't time. 'I know. So walk with me out on the course and we'll chat as we go round,' he replied. Amazing. There's me waiting for Poults to tee off and then walking with him along the fairways with a tape recorder at the ready, pressed to his famous face. Strange interview, I must say. But that's typical of this great of British golfers, who lived up to his nickname that the 'Postman' always delivers.

I've met Poults a few times while covering Opens and I always have to smile when I shake his hand and introduce myself again. It always takes me back to a little story one of the caddies told me some years back when Poults first broke on to the professional circuit.

He was larger than life even back then when one Monday he arrived at the course in a huge limo with the private number plate 'Poults 1'. This audacious sight didn't go unnoticed by the lads in the caddy shack and one went to work on the number plate once the luxury car was parked up for the day. With wit and ingenuity he used black tape and paint to somehow rearrange the wording and comically left the reg plate reading 'Tampax'. Poults, unaware of the caddy skulduggery, innocently drove around for the rest of the week with the embarrassing message emblazoned on the front of the Bentley.

I obviously didn't let the cat out of the bag at our subsequent meetings and I don't think he'd have seen the funny side. But it was a pleasure to meet him and walk the Open courses around Britain with some of the greatest golfers in the world. Tiger Woods, Phil Mickelson, Colin Montgomery, Lee Westwood and Darren Clarke, to mention just a few of the super superstars.

I was privileged, too, to interview, chat and drink with a whole host of footballing legends, with Sir Alex always playing a major part in my journalistic life, as I've mentioned before. Even towards the end of both our careers our paths crossed – with the usual words and eye-piercing stares that were the trademark of one of our greatest-ever football managers.

A couple of years before Fergie retired in 2013 and David Moyes became his successor, relations between the Manchester United manager and the media were strained, to say the least. And, of course, not for the first time. Some of the young journalistic newbies were frankly getting on Fergie's nerves and when he looked at the media men in front of his press conference desk he only recognised a few of the tried and trusted oldies.

Sir Alex became basically unresponsive to questions, and the wicked, mickey-taking sense of humour disappeared for a good chunk of that particular season. So my good mate John Richardson and I decided to take matters into our own hands and had a quiet word with him to see whether we could make peace. Iron out what differences there were between the manager and the media. We followed him down the steps and out of the media centre at the Carrington training ground to confront him at his car. To ask him how we could repair the damage and start again just like the old days.

I'd never seen him go so purple-faced. He was enraged even with two of the so-called good guys. He'd clearly had enough of everyone and anyone from the press corps. Expletives were duly delivered and he furiously got into his car, slamming the door and driving away at speed. But not before I'd managed to utter through his open window, 'Is that a no then, Sir Alex?'

The next week we prepared for the backlash from an enraged Fergie. But he strode into the press conference room, clipped us two round the back of the head and beamed at us as he sat down at the table. He still wasn't responsive to questions, though, although he did try to give Rico and I better answers than he gave to anyone else.

It was a bit like that over at Anfield when Sir Kenny Dalglish was appointed for his second spell as Liverpool manager in 2011. He was always a difficult man to address questions to in a press conference but in this short spell in charge he was even more tight-lipped than before. In fact, it got to the point where he'd grunt and groan at general questions from the floor, give sarcastic replies and only become responsive when Rico and I asked pertinent ones.

Sir Kenny had respect for us and we had respect for him. So much so that we were delighted to later receive an invitation to join him and the likes of Roy Evans, Mark Lawrenson, Steve McMahon, Alan Kennedy and Joe Royle for every pre-Christmas lunch in his favourite Chinese restaurant in Southport. That's an annual get-together now, with me being the lucky, privileged guy to sit next to King Kenny and pull his cracker.

But it wasn't just Manchester United and Liverpool where I found myself in a heady position, although I didn't get off to the best of starts when Blackpool were promoted to the Premier League in 2010.

I'd just returned from the Open at St Andrews and met up with Rico to pop into Blackpool's training ground at Squires Gate in the shadow of the Pleasure Beach's Big One. We went there in the hope of catching a few minutes with the club's own 'Big One' – manager Ian Holloway. After parking up in the training ground car park, we walked towards the modest clubhouse/canteen. But just as we opened the door a burly bodyguard type confronted us after stopping us in our tracks.

'Who the hell are you?' bellowed press officer Matt Williams. We explained we were from the *Daily Star Sunday* and *Sunday Express* and we were there to grab a few minutes with his boss Ian.

'You cheeky b*****ds,' he fumed. 'Would you turn up at Manchester United's training ground unannounced? No, you bloody wouldn't. So F off. You're banned before we even kick a ball in the Premier League.' And with that we were escorted back to our cars and waved off with a V-sign.

We let Matt cool off for a couple of days and then phoned to make the peace. Which we did. After that, Blackpool football club became a regular haunt for the two bad boys who found a way back into their good books. We'd laugh about our Blackpool boot during subsequent years, with Matt becoming a good mate and contact as he moved first to Shrewsbury and then Burnley, which has always had a place in my heart.

Apart from those early *Sunday Mirror* days of summer frolics with the Burnley and Huddersfield boys, my connection at Turf Moor goes back a long way. From being invited to the training ground's weights rooms, working out with a crocked Steve Kindon and Paul Fletcher in the late 70s to a lunch invite from current boss Sean Dyche. Sean kindly showed me around the club's new state-of-the-art training ground, and in every press conference he'd look my way before he started and hold up a huge thumb. Great guy.

Yes, I've been privileged to meet the game's elite – and been fortunate to interview the legends of the past courtesy of the *Daily Star Sunday*'s 'Lunch with a Legend' format, which was a roaring success. The idea was to invite players

One of many ear-bashing moments from the 'Hairdryer' himself, Sir Alex
Ferguson.

Sitting on dad Stan's knee with mum Pat looking on with pride outside married
quarters in RAF Changi.

There's me having a laugh in a box.

Here's me growing up in RAF Oldenburg, getting on my bike

Learning an alphabet which mysteriously only went up to 'P'.

On a day out with mum and dad as my sister Anne takes a quick drink.

Me and grandpa Jack, grandma Kitty and mum in the garden at RAF Oldenburg

Here we are on our wedding day, a young-looking, long-haired Steve and beautiful bride Sylvia outside St John's Church.

One of our many family holidays, this time in Florida with Syl and our lovely young children Nikky and Anthony.

My first taste of journalism at the Stretford and Urmston Journal *with our editorial gang.*

One of many boozy garden parties with the talented editorial team from the Sunday Mirror.

One of my privileged interviews with the legendary Pele, who gladly autographed an England shirt to keep as a souvenir of a remarkable day.

Catching up with one of my many Manchester City heroes Georgi Kinkladze as I interviewed another superstar on his way home to Georgia.

Finally reminiscing with my boyhood footballing rival Kevin Keegan, who is happy to point out who is the real boss.

The next generation. Our beautiful super six grandchildren. How proud am I.

*Our son, Anthony,
playing in the Open.*

*Our first anniversary as
landlord and landlady of The
Antelope Inn at Congleton,
Cheshire.*

and managers from the past to their local pub or restaurant and write anecdotal memories from their glory days.

I remember wining and dining former Manchester United manager Ron Atkinson at his local plush restaurant in the Midlands where he insisted I ordered a bottle of the finest champagne for his wife Maggie. Bit expensive that one but the quality of the stories Big Ron told was priceless.

I met another United legend, goalkeeper Alex Stepney, who, of course, starred in the club's historic 1968 European Cup triumph against Benfica when they became the first English club to win 'Old Big Ears'. We met near his modest home in the village of Hambleton on the Fylde coast and I knew times were hard when he asked if he could have £200 for the interview. The only legend to ask for money. Crying shame really.

I got some great exclusives, too, from those legend lunches. I'll never forget interviewing former Liverpool great Ian Callaghan, who revealed how he'd caught the bus to Anfield for his debut on 16 April 1960. Seemingly he walked to the bus stop with his boots hung over his shoulder and joined the huge queue at the back as the corporation bus arrived. There were hundreds of fans who ushered the debut boy forward to ride to the ground up top.

Ian made me laugh, too, when he revealed a story never told before about the saga of Nobby's Gnashers. The Liverpool winger was in the England squad that was victorious over West Germany in that famous World Cup triumph in 1966. There were no substitutes in those days so Ian entered the Wembley dressing room all suited and booted as a member of the squad to give those England heroes a hearty send-off to the pitch before the greatest victory of their lives.

Nobby Stiles beckoned Ian over before they left the dressing room and took out his false teeth, wrapped them in a handkerchief and handed them to Cally for safe-keeping, saying, 'Can you get them back to me when the game's over?'

Ian stuffed the gnashers into his suit pocket and promised their safe return. The only problem was, of course, that England were triumphant and there was so much celebration that Ian couldn't force his way through the fans to get down to the pitch. That's why film footage of Nobby shows him dancing around the Wembley pitch with that gummy grin, minus his teeth. Hilarious.

But while the column brought the biggest of smiles for most of the time, there was serious sadness too in a few of the legend interviews. Like the time I met with former Manchester City defender Glyn Pardoe at his local near his home in Winsford, Cheshire.

We chatted about those early days of his at Maine Road, where he made his debut in April 1962 at the age of 15 years and 341 days. We talked about his grandson, Tommy Doyle, now earning rave notices himself at the Etihad. And then I asked him about George Best's horror tackle in the 1970 Manchester derby, which left Glyn with a double leg break.

He was adamant that George had meant to do him serious harm with the lunge and revealed how his wife Pat was summoned to his hospital bedside to sign medical forms for an imminent amputation. But in a moment of medical miracles, the club doctor Mr Rose was flown to Manchester from his London clinic just in time to save the leg by reconnecting the blood circulation in the wrecked limb.

Glyn couldn't finish the story as he broke down and sobbed uncontrollably, his shoulders heaving. All I could do was put my arms around him, hug him and wipe his flowing tears. It was a scene of sadness I'll never forget. The pain and trauma still fresh in his mind 50 years after the Best bust-up.

I met up with Glyn a couple of times after that liquid lunch, watching Tommy play superbly for City under-18s and England. A great gentleman, Glyn, someone I'll never forget.

Yes, I met some truly magnificent sportsmen during my career and was honoured to be asked by Welsh football legend Mickey Thomas to co-write his autobiography with my old mate John Richardson. Mickey's was an unbelievable story with some major moments in his life branded on to my memory when penning *Kick-Ups, Hiccups, Lock-Ups*.

There was the time when Mickey was so skint that he'd rip open his mum's settee trying to find coins to buy something to eat. And the real drama away from the pitch when he became involved in a counterfeit currency scam where he laundered money through Wrexham's trainees. He was sentenced to 18 months in jail – although he still argues to this day that he wasn't that guilty.

Anyway, off to the nick he went, with Mickey, as only Mickey could, finding humour in all of his many open prison stays. One in particular, Foston, was a remote unit housing lifers but the prison officers became like his best mates. Every week the friendly officers would take him out for a drink to the pub down the road. I know. Sounds crazy doesn't it?

One night he was with two warders and they got back to the prison to find the gates shut. Instead of being locked up, Mickey was locked outside the jail. So what did they do? Obvious. The prison officers found a ladder, propped it against the gate and Mickey climbed over to get back to his cell. The only man to have ever broken into prison.

I still smile at all Mickey's antics and we're still in touch today, with my heart lifted by his survival after stomach cancer. Good lad Mickey.

Yes, memories are made of this thing called being a journalist. But my own world was about to change when the curtain began falling on my long and, as you can see, eventful career.

CHAPTER 14

IT SEEMED an eternity from the moment I was told on my sunbed that my job was at risk to my eventual departure from the *Daily Star Sunday* and newspapers for good.

I carried on working to my best, dutiful ability amid calls from senior management in May 2019 that I'd now entered a consultation period of 28 days and I had to decide whether to stay or go.

The second day into that legal timeframe came a call from the *Express*'s managing editor Andy Taylor asking me whether I'd made up my mind. I told him that it had only been two days and I hadn't been informed about the terms of the new employment with the Mirror Group owners, now Reach plc.

Within an hour, Taylor had sent me an email with the job description. The role, as expected, was sports reporter for the new Reach empire, which now owned seven national newspapers: the *Daily Mirror, Daily Star, Daily Express, Sunday Mirror, People, Daily Star Sunday* and the *Sunday Express*.

I'd be working mainly for the *Daily Star Sunday* and *Sunday Express*, but where was the answer to the big, big question? Where was the job based? Glancing down the document I soon discovered that the reporting role was in … London. The bloody place I'd resisted residing in on so many occasions in the past.

Quick as a flash I was back on the phone to out-of-his-depth Taylor. 'Andy,' I said. 'I see the new position is based in London. I've turned down jobs there, including the sports editor of the *People*, so many times. I don't want to live in London at this stage of my life.'

'No, no. You don't have to live there,' replied Taylor. 'You could commute. Drive down on a Friday for a press conference and then drive back to the north, returning on a Saturday to do a game.'

Honestly? Are you serious? Driving almost 800 miles in 48-hour return trips? What a joke and an insult to a journalist who had given most of his professional life to newspapers in the Mirror group.

So, not surprisingly, my mind was made up. Deal or no deal? No deal. I'd take the money – what little there was – and leave the industry with my final *Daily Star Sunday* retainer being paid on 2 June 2019. The rest of the consultation period became my notice, basically, and I carried on the best I could, working to the best of my ability until the end. I'd have had it no other way.

The disappointment was that there was no big fuss during my final days. I'd always remembered from my earlier time on the *Sunday Mirror* at Withy Grove in Manchester when anyone left the building for good. They would be 'banged out' in a centuries-old traditional farewell to one of their own. The printers upstairs used to bang on their tables with metal lines of type. Downstairs in the editorial room it was a pounding on the desk with pens, ink bottles … anything to hand.

But Steve Millar was to leave not with a bang but with a whimper. No final goodbye from the office in Bamber Bridge. No farewell drink in Preston with my so-called colleagues. No nothing. Sweet FA. And that's the way it remained with my fellow journos after 17 years' devotion to Express Newspapers. It was almost as if sports editor Michael Ham and the rest of the staff were embarrassed to see me go. Or, more to the point, they couldn't be seen in the company of the old journo who had now become surplus to requirements on the *Daily Star Sunday*.

Thank God I wasn't the great untouchable with my mates outside the office. The likes of Paul Hetherington, John Rico Richardson, Joe Bernstein, Jonathan Northcroft and Steve Bates organised a final drink up at the Town Hall Tavern in Manchester. We talked, as predicted, about the good old days, which were light years away from the current ones in respect of the job – and they were fun.

The enjoyable reminiscing was halted for the presentation, conducted by Joe. I'd no idea how much the lads had donated or what they had bought but I'd an inkling. I fully expected Joe to hand me a plastic bag with a Manchester City shirt inside emblazoned on the back with 'MILLAR 50' to represent my landmark career in journalism.

But no, this is madcap Joe we're talking about. The first farewell gift was a team photograph from what was supposed to be the first time I watched my beloved City – 1890. Oh, how we laughed. Next up was a vanity mirror to represent all my years on the *Mirror*. And a silver star to depict my 17 years on the *Daily Star Sunday*. And a season ticket for my local club Warrington Town, who I've never supported and only visited once since moving to the area 45 years ago.

I was speechless – but not for the reason the old hacks thought. Where was my bloody City shirt with 50 on the back?

Oh well. Onwards and upwards as usual as we headed off for another tried and trusted haunt, Mr Thomas's Chop House, where food and wine were consumed on the outside terrace.

In the end then, a great send-off with a few more pints on the way to the station for the journey home to a new part of my life away from newspapers for the first time since the year it all began, 1968.

There were just 20 miles to home as I looked back on that engrossing, amazing era of mine where from the days of the *Sunday Mirror* to the *Daily Star Sunday* I'd covered football and golf in some incredible, awe-inspiring countries. Work trips all over Europe. From England to Spain, France, Italy, Germany, the Netherlands, Belgium, Poland, Denmark, Norway, Sweden, Turkey, Israel, Russia. From England to Qatar, South Africa, Malaysia, Japan. Thousands and thousands of miles across the globe in the line of duty for my newspapers. But all of a sudden the road to everywhere came to a heart-breaking end of the road.

Those first few days, weeks, of being without a job were hard to handle. The thought of being at home full-time was mind-numbing. Fruitless. I couldn't just settle back into retirement, get the slippers on and wind back in an armchair. I don't even own a pair of slippers.

No, there was still life in the old dog – but no one was prepared to give this one a monetary bone. I was told by my ex-colleagues on the *Mirror* that it would be three years before they could consider re-employing me. Bullshit.

My mate Phil Thomas enquired about freelancing for *The Sun*. Sports editor Shaun Custis was sympathetic, remembering all the help I gave him when he moved to Manchester. But his financial hands were tied concerning hiring new staff.

I hit a brick wall everywhere I enquired. The journalistic shutters were down so I applied for driver jobs, including Click Chemist delivering prescriptions. No one returned my emails. No one got back to me.

I had to do something to combat the boredom so became a voluntary driver for our local hospice in Warrington, St Rocco's. That involved booking in my diary on a Monday the ladies I'd be driving to the hospice and collecting on a Friday. My mind was still active, Mr Ferguson. For two days of the week at least.

But then came the pandemic that began sweeping the country in March 2020 and my wheels fell off again with no pick-ups, no drop-offs for obvious reasons as COVID-19 threatened the lives of the very lovely ladies I was driving.

So what the hell could I do with myself amid all this mayhem? Get the old grey stuff working. No, not my hair. The brain. So life changed again as I remembered the past as clearly and lucidly as if it was today. The struggle was recalling with accuracy what the hell happened yesterday.

But I think I managed it, with the Millarman bringing the family up to date on everything that I was fortunate enough to experience during my existence on this planet.

Life, though, as they say, still goes on.

CHAPTER 15

SO HERE we are amid this terrible pandemic that has blighted 2020 and 2021, and life for me has gone full circle. The 'Fifty Shades of Going Grey' has now been well and truly chronicled as I've unearthed milestone after milestone on the Millar journey through the ages of my time here on earth. But along the 'grey' adventure there are black-and-white recollections that pierce my heart even to this day.

Why, after meeting the love of my life in Sylvia, did I treat her with such contempt and disdain in my teenage years? I can still feel the flutter from within when I set eyes on Sylvia for that very first time. She was the only one for me as our dates in the Blue Rooms in Sale, Cheshire, grew into a relationship that was destined for a loving future. Yet time and time again I acted like a complete idiot.

When our love was growing and blooming I cruelly cut it off at the roots. Sylvia was in love with me and that was undoubtedly reciprocated in myself. So why the hell did I treat her so badly in those early years?

I know I took the death of my father Stan to heart. His sudden passing ripped a chunk out of my own at just 19.

But that was no valid excuse for plunging the dagger into Sylvia's heart with those endless dumpings without notice. I never knew how much I hurt her. Couldn't comprehend how many times I devastated her innocent mind and body. She bloody didn't deserve that and I acted like a cold-hearted fool.

Sylvia's pain was there for all to see these 50 years later after clearing out our loft. She discovered letters written to me from her bedroom. One was dated 7 September 1970 and penned at 1am from 73 Wendover Road, Brooklands. She said:

> Dearest Stephen. I think I am going absolutely crazy cos I don't know what I am even writing to say. But I know Steve you won't hold it against me (I hope).
>
> I haven't heard from you for quite a while. I suppose by now you have forgotten all about me haven't you. But I'm afraid I cannot say the same about you. Although I have tried time and time again to forget you Steve it's just no use. You are with me every minute of time.
>
> I don't know quite how to word what I wish to say exactly but here I go. Please try not to laugh. I have been meaning to ask you Steve all the months that I have been going out with you just when you felt like it.
>
> There is just no getting away from the fact that you have messed me about. Admittedly I say it is my own fault. But I just like to know where I

stand as it is now seven months since you finished with me properly – January 23.

You must probably think I am absolutely mad but please try to see my point Steve. I do love you.

There was another emotional letter Syl unearthed, which read:

It began at a club in Timperley called Kersall's. I was absolutely crazy about a boy called Steve Millar – and so was my friend Sandra.

I thought Sandra would get Steve because he always asked her to do the limbo. So then the night came when Steve said to me: Will you go out with me? I just casually said yes. He just grabbed hold of me and kissed me for so long I thought he'd never let go. I felt as though I was walking on air.

I really grew to love Steve genuinely but he finished with me on a Sunday night at the Locarno in Sale. I was so upset. There were so many times he finished and still to this day I haven't heard from him.

But I still love him and I wait for the day to come when Steve will love me and we shall get married. The end.

Well, thank God it wasn't the end and I eventually came to my senses and married the girl I've always loved. And always will for the rest of my life.

I hadn't read those letters until now, on Syl's return trip from loft duties. She'd never posted them to me but even if I'd received them all those years ago I probably would have been daft enough not to react in the right way.

But now, after beating myself up, here we are heading for that golden wedding anniversary that I could never have imagined all those years ago as that junior reporter covering such marital magical moments. Still together. Husband and wife. Syl and Steve – a loving combination no man, or woman, will ever put asunder. Ever.

It could have been so different, though, if Syl hadn't been so patient and understanding with a fool like me messing with her emotions.

So here we are, so immensely proud that we've journeyed to this point in our lives together and comforted by the dynasty we've produced from a lifetime of happily married bliss. We have two wonderful children in Nikky and Anthony. Obviously all grown up with families of their own and settled into their lovely homes in Woolston, Warrington.

Nikky, a lecturer at Warrington Vale Royal College, is supported as ever by the man in her life, cement plant manager Andy. They, like me and Syl, cherish the children brought into the Bradley world.

First George, who at 16 is destined for an academically brilliant and breathtaking future. His grades at school in every subject are in A-star heaven and he's been accepted for a place at Winstanley College in Wigan to study physics and maths. And they're happy to put him on the waiting list for Oxbridge. Wow.

And then completing the Bradley household, not forgetting pet dog Buster of course, are our 12-year-old twin granddaughters Daisy and Molly, who are excelling in their own favoured subjects at King's Academy, Woolston. Daisy loves her geography, and Molly – who now likes to be known as Mollie – is into drama big-time, so watch out for future appearances on *Coronation Street*. They're both pretty and petite but don't be fooled by innocent appearances. On the football pitch they won't duck any physical issue and man-of-the-match awards are in the same abundance as tackling, shooting and scoring.

Just down the road in Woolston reside the Millar family. Son Anthony, who is the successful and popular professional at Ellesmere Golf Club, Worsley, and wife Clare, an early health triage worker.

Their son William, aged ten, is the eldest, nearing the end of his early education at Woolston C of E Primary School just a short walk away from home. Maths is his favoured subject but he's earned top marks outside school for his football and rugby league skills. What a goalkeeper and what a tackler in the oval ball game. It takes your breath away just watching. Oh, and don't forget golf. His swing and ball striking even at his early age are a chip off the old block.

His beautiful sister Sophie, at eight, loves her maths, too. But she's into modern language and is top of the class for art, with a Blue Peter badge being a fitting reward for her work with letters – and helping her mum out.

Then last but not least is Harry, who has a place in the heart of everyone he meets. It's been heart-breaking in this COVID-19 nightmare that Gramps and Grandma haven't been able to get our rightful quota of hugs and kisses from the little man. But we will catch up one day soon in showering him in love and emotion as Harry grows into another special child in our grandkid dynasty.

Even at such a tender age Harry's an avid bird-watcher and made his childminder Clare double up with laughter when she quizzed him as to what was his favourite bird. Without hesitation, he answered. 'It's a Robin ... but daddy loves tits.' Hilarious. Talk about out of the mouths of babes.

What hasn't been quite so funny is the damn virus. The unprecedented restrictions and lockdowns have resulted in limited contact with family members over these endless, mind-numbing months. It's a fate suffered by the entire country as the pandemic continued to threaten the whole of the UK and the rest of the world all the way into the New Year of 2022.

But while it's all so very different from the norm, I'll still raise a regular glass or six to my wonderful family.

And to my sister Anne, who at Christmas 2019 was given just three months to live as a return of cancer ravaged her body. To say she's been a fighter is the understatement of all time. Anne survived beyond the 27 March birthday she never thought she'd see, and after endless stays in hospitals and hospices, our kid is still staying strong beyond belief. She's always had her husband Ian by her side, night and day, with the brother-in-law I could do without in the starting line-up as player manager of Carrington AFC back in the day.

Roll on all those decades and Ian has become the undisputed man of their particular match as carer supreme. I say constantly by her side but that was until the turn of the year when Ian was taken to hospital with a suspected heart attack. After examination, it was discovered he had a faulty heart valve but constant nose bleeds seriously delayed his operation.

It's at this stage that I start preparing to sign off this 'Fifty Shades of Going Grey' with a reminder to myself of all those good times I've had in my professional life.

As well as discovering those love letters from 50 years ago, Syl unearthed a couple of black-and-white photographs too, of my journalistic past. The first is a snap of me interviewing footballing legend Pelé when he opened Dave Whelan's JJB sports warehouse in Wigan in 1996 – 30 years after I'd wave to the samba superstar as his Brazil team coach drove through Partington in that famous World Cup year. Pelé even did me the honour of signing an England shirt provided by Dave with his sought-after signature taking pride of place beneath the Three Lions badge.

And then out of a dusty handbag came a photograph of my mental mentor Sir Alex in a familiar pose. Staring angrily straight at yours truly with a wagging finger, making some point or other that I was on the receiving end of another ban.

Good old days. Missed greatly by my heavy heart. But there will always be a smile on my face too, as I live with my memories of the family, friends – and enemies – I've encountered on this incredible journey through life.

The phone calls have dried up. No surprise there. Heard nothing from the office since the day I left and only contact with Rico, Paul Hetho, Stengun, Phil Thomas, Joe Bernstein and Colin Mafham has kept me going through these strange months of retirement.

But the old brainbox worked overtime just recently when I received a call out of the *sacre bleu* from a French journalist I've never met, Florian Lefevre, who in October 2020 was writing a feature on Blackburn's 1995 Premier League title triumph. He'd interviewed two of Rovers' title-winning heroes, Colin Hendry and Mike Newell, but for some unknown reason wanted to focus on that fabulous final Friday before the Sunday triumph when the media met Sir Kenny Dalglish's 'backroom' staff and got hammered – both on the pitch and off it. I recounted my memories of that unforgettable one-sided meeting of manager and media, when us journalists were the butt of every Blackburn joke.

And all those years later I received another quip from Sir Kenny after I'd texted the Kop idol with a good luck message following his admission to hospital with the dreaded coronavirus. His reply was lightning quick, just like his feet and, as always, in reference to that 16-0 Blackburn staff victory over us journalists and me in goal desperately trying to get my Schmeichel goalie gloves on every damn shot I faced.

Sir Kenny said simply: 'Thank you for the text. You must have dictated it as I thought your fingers were smashed.' Smiling emoji, smiling emoji, smiling emoji. Enough said.

CHAPTER 16

I'M SO privileged to have known King Kenny over all those years, from fabulous player, opponent in that Blackburn vs Press match to trophy-winning manager and now Liverpool ambassador. Now I'm retired our meetings are few and far between, with the pandemic barring my entry to Anfield for too many long months.

King Kenny is, though, still my next-door neighbour on the table at our Christmas Chinese lunches in Southport, where food isn't the only thing on everyone's lips. Catching up on the past and hearing some previously unmentioned anecdotes in the company of Joe Royle, Phil Neal, Mark Lawrenson and co. is a real recipe for a successful day out.

Yes, from those early *Sunday Mirror* days, being privileged to have sat in Bob Paisley's bungalow watching football, I've always had strong connections to Liverpool. Never a love affair, you understand, because of my Manchester City allegiance, but being in the company of Bob, King Kenny and co. brought me close to the club from Anfield.

But our relationship was seriously strained on the Champions League night that City's coach was bombarded with bottles, stones and flares before their quarter-final loss in April, 2018. City had been asked to change the normal route to the stadium because Liverpool were concerned about fans' safety, with buildings along the journey adorned with scaffolding. The club were worried that their own supporters could fall off the scaffolding if they got too boisterous.

So City obliged and journeyed along the other end of Stanley Park – a detour posted by police on their social media platform. All along the new route were so-called supporters who threw everything they could at the City coach, causing broken windows and seriously worrying the on-board players, manager Pep Guardiola and his staff.

Inside Anfield the atmosphere was more than intimidating and I admit that I was verbally abused for the one-and-only time in a press box. When Liverpool scored their third, one 'supporter' raced towards me and spat out hatred of the Manchester enemy. I begged for help from watching stewards but they hurriedly turned their back on this seriously frightened reporter.

That incident will never detract from my relationship with Kenny, though. I'm truly honoured to have known both him and Sir Alex. Two of the legendary, iconic figures in the history of our wonderful game.

Okay, as I've said, there were moments of madness and angry exchanges, leading to those bans from Manchester United ordered by a purple, raging boss of one of the greatest clubs on the planet. But overall I like to believe that this hugely successful manager in the world of football, with 38 trophies in his ram-jammed cabinet, had an abundance of respect for me and a handful of my colleagues in the day. The likes of John Richardson, Bill Thornton, Peter Fitton and David Walker.

It was evident after more than 20 years of working with Sir Alex that he did appreciate the older guys on the sports writing scene. I've lost count of the number of times he'd call for me, Fitton and Walker after landing at a foreign European airport before yet another Champions League match. Fergie would address us by the baggage drop and stress the point that he hoped the referee in charge of the following night's match in Italy, Spain or wherever would be strong enough not to be fooled by play-acting on the pitch practised by the opposition. Sure enough, Sir Alex would get the publicity he required on the morning of the match in our respective tabloids and the feedback to the referee's room would always ensure a fair whistle display.

It was the same after that historic Champions League triumph over Bayern Munich in the Camp Nou in '99. It was myself and the fellow dinosaurs Fergie sought out after that sensational victory to arrange a meeting the following day at the team-based Arts Hotel in Barcelona to pour out his emotions from that historic night.

Fergie had no time for the young bucks of the day and said so in his autobiography, *Alex Ferguson: My Autobiography*. As par for the course, the then United manager didn't hold back on his contempt for the younger breed of sports journalists who began attending his press conferences in scruffy, casual clobber. His respect only focused on the older, more established men in jackets and ties.

Sir Alex said:

> Latterly we had a lot of young reporters who dressed more casually than the men I had known in my early years. Maybe it was a generational thing but it just didn't sit well with me. It's a difficult job for those young reporters because they are under so much pressure from their editors.
>
> So there was an intensity and volatility about the modern media I found difficult. When I first came to Manchester, I was wary of some but wasn't guarded in the way I was in my final years.
>
> Characters like John Bean and Peter Fitton were decent lads. Bill Thornton, David Walker, Steve Millar. Decent guys.

To be called 'decent' by the legend who managed Manchester United for 25 years is a never-to-be-forgotten accolade that remains with me to this day after surviving for two decades in the Fergie firing line.

I emerged unscathed with a bottomless pit of memories from my time with Fergie, Kenny and all those wonderful players, managers and pressmen from the past who made my journalistic life worth living.

Fifty years in the game has certainly been one hell of a ride and one I could never have contemplated when I began my career covering inquests and golden weddings on the *Stretford and Urmston Journal.*

It's so hard to believe I'm here at this precious moment in my time. To still have a brain functioning as normal to recall the wonderful experiences of the past. But as I said earlier, that advice from Sir Alex to keep the grey matter working at full pace has paid off perfectly in recording my private and professional life from the days of being born in Changi to where I am today.

Retirement hasn't come easy, and as I entered my second year of walking along the canal bank during a pandemic, I was finally coming to terms with not working for a living. Or sitting in a press box. Or flying halfway across the world to cover World Cups and Champions League encounters.

I've really come down to earth – but not with a bump. I'm content in retirement. Picking up a generous old age pension and remembering pulling match report intros out of a hat – and pulling pints in the Antelope at Congleton. I've achieved more in life than I thought was ever possible. A seriously proud husband, brother, dad and gramps, with a family dynasty that swells my heart every minute of every day.

It's remarkable to reach this point in my life where I've just passed the 70-year-old birthday landmark with a celebration garden party with the family, my sister Anne and her husband Ian. The following night it was dinner with Syl, Nikky, Anthony, Andy and Clare in our favourite Italian, where my generous (like me) son picked up the whopping bill.

We had fun, which took my mind off coming face to face with all those three score years and ten banners and balloons that adorned our Grappenhall home courtesy of Syl. It's only a number, I was reminded constantly. Yes, but it's a bloody big number and one I'm slowly coming to terms with as I look forward to whatever the future has to hold.

Whatever happens, though, I've got my wonderful family by my side with another recent reminder that life for me has come full circle.

It came when Clare asked me to pick up little Harry after his new school taster afternoon at Woolston C of E Primary. So, mask on, I waited for his happy, angelic face to appear at the classroom door – standing in the same playground where I'd waited to pick up Nicky 44 years previously, followed by Anthony. They say time flies but that's at turbo-booster rocket pace.

So Harry at the age of four started big school in September 2021. Brother William left Woolston Primary School for King's Academy to join twin granddaughters Daisy and Molly. Sophie is growing up quickly at Woolston Primary and George started Winstanley College for the next stage of his amazing education. There go the rockets again.

Yes, it's been an amazing summer of 2021 with my team Manchester City being crowned champions of England – again. Winning the Carabao Cup for the fourth successive season and agonisingly losing the Champions League Final to a team I'm not going to mention. Oh, and England, surprise, surprise, lost in a penalty shoot-out to Italy in the Euro 2020 Final at the start of what would be a memorable summer.

I was transfixed by the Open Championship, which, for the first time, made me seriously envious that I couldn't be there in the media tent at the Royal St George's Golf

Club at beautiful Sandwich. I'd have given my right arm to have turned back the clock and be walking that wonderful course, reporting on the sport I adore.

My mind flicked back to ten years before at the same wonderful venue where the *Daily Star Sunday* for once did me and Tony Stenson justice by hiring us a beachside cottage at Broadstairs where Syl and Stengun's wife Carol joined us for a memorable week. As usual the Gun and I worked hard and played hard at Sandwich, where I enjoyed another July birthday treat with the two girls. Little did I know that ten years later I'd be shoved permanently outside that media tent looking in.

That's when you begin to think about all the old good times, as I have throughout these pages. All the milestones and memories. The privileges of being in the same company as many of the sporting greats.

None more so than Sir Alex, of course, who had given permission for a documentary to be produced back in 1998 tracing his life from a schoolboy in Govan, Glasgow, to his apprenticeship in the shipyard, to becoming one of the greatest football managers of all time. I was alerted to this historic gem and found it on YouTube recently.

I watched with huge interest as the documentary travelled through time until the cameras focused on the build-up to United's Champions League quarter-final clash with AS Monaco at Old Trafford in the March. The centre of attention was Fergie at his pre-match conference, facing the world's press with yours truly standing to his left, notebook in hand. I remember thinking how smart I looked with jacket, shirt and tie. A dress code I always adhered to when on the journalistic job for all those 50 years and one Sir Alex approved of. Or so I thought.

My question, I reasoned, would begin to fill the following morning's back pages, with Sir Alex sure to respond. Was it time, I asked, for the Old Trafford-packed house to become United's 12th man and roar their heroes on to another memorable Euro victory.

I waited for his tub-thumping response. But no words left his lips. Instead, Sir Alex slowly shook his head, smiled broadly and brought the official UEFA press conference to a halt with a huge chuckle. He pointed directly at my red floral tie and, for the first time, was lost for words. Instead, he just poked fun at the designer statement, mumbled, 'That tie, that tie,' and took several minutes to compose himself and carry on. The only time in UEFA history that a journalist had tied a manager up in knots.

And that's the one-on-one tomfoolery I miss to this day. Being in the company of a great and enjoying every single millisecond of the banter. But I've got to shake off the nostalgia and look to the future. A future with my family as, instead of jetting off to Portugal, the 12 of us journeyed for a staycation like millions of other pandemic-hit Brits. We went to the lovely Isle of Wight for a week's stay in a beautiful woodland mansion in Ventnor, where we had endless family fun and frolics to swell the 70-year-old heart of old Gramps.

Boy was that break needed, coming a week after Syl and I had moved into our new bungalow retreat back near our old homes in Woolston, Warrington. It was a return prompted by Nikky and Anthony, who wanted Mum and Dad to be nearer our two wonderful families. So we sold our Grappenhall home for £265,000 and Nikky and Anthony invested in our new £250,000 bungalow across Woolston Park in Paddington.

I must say it was a huge wrench leaving East View in Grappenhall after 18 wonderful, happy years in our beautiful home. But moving nearer the kids and grandchildren as the old legs start to grow old and weary was a sensible decision. Probably the first time Syl and I have thought like that after so many married years of living life on an impulse.

It's from our newly renovated bungalow lounge that I pen the final words of my life story. As I look out on a different view from a place we now call home. It's a new adventure, which looked impossible to savour during the two nightmare days of when we should have moved only to be blocked by a solicitor who raised legal objections on behalf of her client, a madcap move that almost saw us repack the van and head back to Grappenhall.

But in the end sanity prevailed. Every legal box was ticked and, after a never-to-be-forgotten weekend of attempting to slow down this old heart of mine, the completion day finally arrived. And here we are now, surrounded by our wonderful family and already planning a return soon to our holiday heaven, where this time there will be no bolt out of the Algarve blue.

No sports editor. No managing editor. No other editorial numbskull can touch me now. I'm free to cherish this wonderful life provided by dear old Stan and Pat and look forward to the rest of my life surrounded by Millar and Bradley generations.

BOB BAYLISS

*(Stretford and Urmston Journal and
Sunday Mirror)*

I WORKED with Steve at the *Stretford and Urmston
Journal* at the start of our journalistic careers and later we
became colleagues at the *Sunday Mirror* in Manchester.
But those early days in the *Journal* office were so special for
both of us. We were young and raw recruits but boy what
a good grounding we received to start us on the journey to
what seemed a lifetime in national newspapers.

I worked closely with Steve covering all aspects of the
job – court cases, golden weddings and inquests – every
local story you could think of as we learned our trade under
the guidance of our respected editor Maurice Brown.

Every Wednesday, though, I assumed a different role
– as chauffeur to Mr Millar as we travelled to Bolton
in the early hours when the *Journal* was printed at the
Bolton Evening News. So yes, it was my job to pick
him up from the Millar family home in Partington, a
Manchester overspill estate. I lived in Urmston and to

me Partington was this lawless Wild West town with too few sheriffs.

Situated on the other side of the River Mersey, the estate had been created to house mainly Manchester city dwellers who had been forced out by a police chief's religious policy of shutting down city centre life. Pubs and clubs in particular. In short, it was a place where many of its residents didn't want to be.

Partington had a reputation that filled me with trepidation on every visit. To journey there in the very early hours, well, what terrors could I expect? Could my car end up on bricks? But despite this and the other fears, my biggest dread of arriving late for the appointment at the *Bolton Evening News* always won over.

I often found myself mega early and sitting in wait outside Steve's home at 6 Forsythia Walk. Parked in a side road. Lights off. Hunkered down waiting, waiting.

'Come on Steve, come on Steve,' I'd whisper. Is he up yet? What if I'm approached by some stranger? Doesn't look good sat alone in my Ford Anglia car very early doors with lights out.

Then phew, the bathroom light blinks on. He's up. Phew, the end is in sight. More minutes tick by though. What the hell is he doing? We're going to be bloody late.

Finally, Steve emerges (pretty much on time I have to say) and I can finally unlock the passenger door.

The early exchange was always the same. 'Been waiting long?' says Steve.

'No,' I always lied. 'Only just got here.' Here's hoping the engine starts. I need to escape Dodge City. Like now.

And we always did, to hit the road and the motorway to get to the *Bolton Evening News* – always on time. We saw the pages into print and then gobbled piled-high plates of toast from the canteen before heading to our Urmston office. The *Journal* was ready to be read by our weekly readers.

Just a few years later, our paths crossed again on the *Sunday Mirror*, with both of us climbing up the ladder in the national newspaper world. I sat a few yards away from Steve, who by that time was heavily involved in his sports writing, while I concentrated on my news and feature production duties.

We worked hard and, as Steve has said, played hard too. Well, the sports desk certainly did. Some of their lunches lasted longer than our working day, with those lengthy Friday trips to Sam's Chop House in the city centre going down in boozy history.

I remember vividly the weeks leading up to one particular Christmas and everyone in the office was rapidly getting into the true spirit of the festive season. No more so than when the high-spirited sports lads came back from yet another extended lunch, having discovered a recently-opened joke shop in the adjacent Arndale shopping precinct. Several jolly japes ensued but came to a crashing end one particular lunchtime with an incident previously described by Steve and one I'll never, ever forget.

Wendy Cuerden, the news desk secretary, was a lovely lady, if not a little high and mighty, despite her diminutive frame. Strict and efficient was our Wendy, a no-nonsense type who believed the news operation was far superior to sport or us in features/production. Her desk, outside the news editor's cubicle, meant she had her back to the rest of the office. Therefore, she was a prime target for Steve and his sports desk pranksters.

Looping droplets of water began to fall on Wendy's head from up high, carefully targeted by various joke shop water pistol devices fired from Steve's 'Department of High Jinks'. This went on randomly for several days until, as we came back from lunch, four burly maintenance men were present, suitably tooled-up, discussing how to take apart the false ceiling above Wendy's desk to find the rogue leaking pipe, which, of course, never existed.

Unsurprisingly, things then went very quiet from the direction of the sports desk. Bottom drawers were cleared and various water shooting devices were smuggled from the premises, never to be seen again.

From that moment, visits to the joke shop weren't as frequent and for a while we had peace with a capital 'P' in the office. Except in the case of the editor's Christmas 'feet'. But then that's another story in the wonderful, comical – and always professional – life of Steve Millar.

JOHN HUXLEY

(Sunday Mirror)

FORMER US President Thomas Jefferson had it that 'all men are created equal'. Well, all I can say is that he didn't have the opportunity of meeting Steve Millar.

History afforded me that opportunity in November 1977 when I joined the *Sunday Mirror*'s sports staff in Manchester. It's at that point that equality becomes a moot point.

Despite earning my spurs in my chosen profession, serving in what might best be called an 'on-job apprenticeship' working for a freelance journalist and then at two provincial evening newspapers, I actually knew very little. Certainly far less than Steve.

Steve was one of nine other journalists either working in or linked to the paper's sports desk in Manchester. Five, including Steve, were based in the labyrinth newspaper plant, Thomson House, in Manchester's Withy Grove.

Having progressed up what was certainly a more traditional route to attaining national newspaper employment, Steve had developed into what any cricket team would have given their eye teeth for – a good all-rounder. Even in his late twenties he possessed a well-defined nose for a good story. An eye for pleasing page design and a gut that could withstand more than several bottles of Holsten Pils at one session. Thus, he was perfectly equipped for a journey up the higher echelons of sports journalism.

Now, just in case I'm in danger of fashioning an impression that Steve was close to perfection, let me strike a note of caution. Journalistically he might have been. But, dear reader, he had another talent too. An aptitude for leading me, and others, socially astray.

Joining the *Mirror* staff in Manchester had returned me to my native city but, as I've already told you, I was far from the finished article journalistically. Quite a few corners still needing removing and Steve, despite being seven years younger than me, went about the task with alacrity. My unsophisticated sub-editing skills were totally and regularly exposed and he almost enjoyed reshaping my story copy. I could, however, stand all that because he was making me into a better journalist, even within the demanding atmosphere of a red-top tabloid newspaper.

But what I wasn't prepared for was Steve's encouragement for me to dramatically increase my capacity for alcohol.

When I left the comfort of the *Huddersfield Daily Examiner* to join the *Sunday Mirror*, my confirmation interview with Tony Smith, the paper's national sports editor in London, had descended into an alcoholic adventure that has served me well when I've been called upon to recount my time with a national newspaper.

Such was the post-interview hangover that I promised myself I'd never, I repeat never, drink that much again. How little did I know what was to happen next.

Within three weeks of me joining the *Sunday Mirror* staff I discovered that Steve was organising a staff trip to the Guinness distribution depot not far from his home town of Warrington, Cheshire.

'You'd love to go wouldn't you Hux?' he asked. You have to understand here that the question was far more a demand that I put in an appearance than an invitation.

I was the department's 'new boy' so I accepted the 'invitation'. There was no way I was going to be a party-pooper. I lived near Huddersfield in West Yorkshire, so on the appointed day I blagged a lift from my then wife, Carol, to the town's railway station and made my way to the Manchester office.

A hired minibus arrived to carry us all to Runcorn, where we enjoyed a quick trip around the Guinness plant and then hit the tasting room to consume copious amounts of Guinness and its associated products.

After lunch, the *Mirror* party moved on to the Red Lion pub in Preston Brook to maintain the flow of alcohol. At around 4.30pm the landlord threw us out claiming, 'I'm open again in half an hour and I haven't had my tea.' But he wasn't all bad, selling us half bottles of Bell's whisky to keep us going on the way back to Manchester.

Sufficient to say my good intentions of not consuming my interview proportions of alcohol were completely trashed. Like me. On top of falling out of the rear doors of the minibus when it stopped at some traffic lights in

Manchester city centre, my train journey back to West Yorkshire was spent fighting waves of nausea in the train's toilet.

Such was the height of my hangover the following morning that I had to ask Carol to call the office, saying that I must have eaten something that hadn't suited me. That didn't fool anybody. But I did make it to the office that day, eventually walking through the doors at around 4pm to a round of applause.

What an adventure, you might say. And I wouldn't disagree. But why should Steve Millar take the blame for your own bad behaviour, you might ask?

Well, having arranged the Guinness end of the deal, the transport and collected the monies due, he didn't go. He pulled out at the eleventh hour claiming that he had family duties to perform.

This, as I discovered, started a trend. Steve, and his partner in any enterprise, Bill Thornton, would have an idea for a great trip. I'd be roped into the scheme but, by some mysterious means I still don't understand even 40 years later, I'd end up making the arrangements and adding to my collection of hangovers.

Steve also possessed sporting prowess as well as a journalistic talent. He enjoyed playing football as well as reporting on it. To that he added playing golf. Once a year he played in a tournament organised by *Daily Express* sports writer Alan Thompson at Huddersfield Golf Club. Steve recruited me as his caddie.

To be fair, I didn't mind. It was certain to be a great day. The weather wasn't too bad and the promise of a splendid post-golf meal made it an attractive proposition. But what Steve hadn't taken into account was that I didn't know anything about the genteel sport of golf – or its established etiquette. Thus, equipped with Steve's bag of clubs, I stood at the first tee watching my 'client' prepare himself for the contest to come.

That was when the trouble started. Steve went to make his first shot. He placed the ball upon the tee and then looked demandingly at me. I didn't move. There was no way I was going to make a faux pas. Steve then walked over to me and said, 'Well ... give me a club.' I picked one out of the bag and gave it to him. An expression of fear creased his bearded face. 'Hux,' he screamed, 'that's a bloody putter. Give me that driver.' At least he pointed to the club he wanted this time.

Not a great start. But we reached the sixth hole and Steve's drive had landed squarely on the fairway. His second shot had reached well into the green. As we walked up to the edge of the green, I thought he said, 'Tend the flag,' so I picked the flag pole out of the hole and put it back in gently. Steam was metaphorically coming out of Steve's ears. 'Hux, I said attend the flag. Don't you know anything?' All he'd wanted me to do was stand next to the flag and take it out of the hole if his putt showed signs of dropping in.

[This is where Hux is confused and must have had a hip flask in the bag that day. What actually happened is that I asked him: 'Tend please,' as I began lining up my putt. He rooted in the bag and instead of the putter handed me a ten-iron. Now back to Hux...]

My lack of golfing etiquette or knowledge had clearly put the mockers on his expectations. His first putt drifted at pace to the right of the hole. His second not only sped by the hole on a downhill slope but the ball also stopped a good distance further away than where he'd first started. The tension broke after his third putt skirted the lip of the hole and sped on across the green. Steve swung his putter around his head several times, uttering curses and lamentations before letting it fly out of his hand into the surrounding trees and bushes.

'That's your fault Hux,' he steamed. 'You'd better go find it now.' Glad to escape the rising tide of wrath, I did as I was asked. But could I find it? No, of course I couldn't, and eventually it took Steve, his fellow players and I to locate it lodged in a bush.

During the search several parties had overtaken our group while we scrabbled in the woods and they couldn't wait to get back to the clubhouse to reveal our alleged 'lost ball' search. But, as was nearly always the case, we learned to laugh at ourselves and the story of the 'flying putter' grew better with every passing drink during the evening-long celebratory dinner.

Steve and I were part of the same close-knit departmental team for 11 years before Robert Maxwell disbanded us. We'd remember many, many amazing adventures. Drank much beer and wine. Shared triumphs and occasional failures and emerged with a friendship that has stood the test of time.

We've stood together at the funeral services of former colleagues. Supported each other during times of strife. And I shall never forget Steve's generosity in offering me shifts at sports desks he controlled as I struggled to establish myself as a freelance journalist after the Maxwell butchery of May 1988.

Good times and bad times, we saw it through. No doubt Steve will sub-edit this, my contribution. And there's every chance I won't recognise it when the book is published. But the one thing I'll know is that it will read better. That's just how it was for 11 years and I don't expect anything to have changed even 34 years later.

BILL THORNTON

I WAS 38 years a tabloid sports hack and, in all that time, I never met a more able, enthusiastic and talented 'small-sheet' journalist than my friend Steve Millar. Steve oozed tabloid from the moment I met him when he joined the *Sunday Mirror* in Manchester more than 40 years ago and his first question was: 'Bill, what's the expenses situation here?'

And boy was the exes situation good in those halcyon days at Mirror Group. As with so many other aspects of life then at Withy Grove, the generosity of the exes 'pinky' system – when you presented a pink slip signed by your departmental boss that entitled you to cash in hand in lieu of your exes – was something I probably didn't appreciate until Robert Maxwell brought the whole operation to a shuddering end.

Steve and I took full advantage of the pinkies as we took the opportunity to enjoy the famous (occasionally infamous) two-to-three-hour lunches, most notably our regular Friday sojourns to Sam's Chop House in Manchester.

Steve not only had a prodigious appetite for fun and mischievous humour but also for lager, the goddess Stella being his favoured tipple, as I recall. Although this favourite was to be superseded by red wine in later years. In fact, I reckon he pioneered the practice of putting red wine in the fridge. When last orders were called, Steve invariably requested two, sometimes three, bottles of Stella. And, if it wasn't his round, he'd always offer to pay for the extras.

But it didn't matter how much Steve consumed, his work was never affected ... and what an operator he was. I'd be surprised if our sports editor Peter Shaw would disagree when I say that Steve was the best appointment he made.

Our new recruit quickly established himself as a top all-rounder. Someone possessed of ideas, imagination, page-scheming ability and a slick, punchy writing style. I can only think that it was this impressive collection of qualities that proved too much for the egotistical future sports editor Des Kelly, who forced Steve out of the *Daily Mirror* many years down the line. More of that later.

Steve and I enjoyed many a laugh and some bizarre experiences. None more so than when one of his many hang-ups – which included never fastening the top button of his shirt and a fixation about eating anything that wasn't prepared by himself or his wife Sylvia – was his fear of flying. That phobia forced us to abandon a Belfast-bound aircraft on the tarmac in the Isle of Man. We'd flown out of Manchester en route to the Northern Ireland Football Writers' Association annual dinner and Steve was in white-knuckle mode as he gripped the arms of the seat at take-off.

So imagine our surprise – and his horror – when the plane started to descend within minutes. For reasons I can't recall, we had to touch down on the Isle of Man as part of the schedule. The prospect of another take-off and landing was bad enough for Steve to ponder. Even worse was when we thundered down the runway again and came to a screeching, shuddering halt before heading back to the terminal following a stark few minutes' silence before the pilot reported a technical fault.

Steve had had enough. 'Bill, I've got to get off,' he said, white-faced. It was obvious he meant it so I summoned the stewardess, who sympathised. We requested the opening of the hold from which we retrieved our golf bags and other luggage under the quizzical gaze of our fellow passengers. As we trooped into the terminal building – I'll admit to being happy to have got off myself – we were approached by two guys who turned out to be airport security, who wanted an explanation as to why we'd abandoned a Belfast flight at the height of the Troubles.

'Did you see that thing doing an emergency stop?' we asked before explaining the purpose of our flight. The 'cops' readily accepted our explanation that Steve had a morbid fear of flying, one of them admitting he'd have got off too. Especially when it was revealed that the plane had carried out an emergency stop to prevent hitting a small plane that had crossed its path at the critical moment of take-off.

So we telephoned our excuses to our colleague and dinner host Bill Clark in Belfast, booked into a poky hotel and that night watched the unfolding drama of the Israel Embassy siege in London – accompanied by Steve's usual stash of Stella bottles.

On another occasion, he and I entertained former England centre-forward Joe Royle, then Oldham Athletic manager, to a lunch in Manchester at which Steve and I got so inebriated we ended up in the hotel swimming pool in our underpants. Joe wisely remained at the poolside table, sipping his drink and diverting his eyes from the embarrassment in the water.

Then there was the time I was walking down the first fairway at Valderrama on the final day of the 1997 Ryder Cup, following the singles match between Ian Woosnam and Fred Couples in my *Daily Star* days. Steve, then on the *Mirror*, walked across and said he'd like to introduce me to someone he'd met. A moment later a buggy drove over and out jumped former US President George Bush, greeting me with a pumping handshake and the words: 'Bill, any friend of Steve's is a friend of mine.' Seemingly they had formed an unlikely friendship walking the course together earlier that day.

Once the president's armed-to-the-teeth bodyguards had accepted we were no threat, I was also introduced to former First Lady Barbara Bush and we went on to witness Woosie's 8&7 thrashing in the company of US 'royalty'. Great stuff.

Steve and I never worked on the same sports desk following the demise of the *Sunday Mirror*'s Manchester operation in 1988 when he first formed a freelance agency partnership with Alan Nixon and then became sports editor of the newly formed *Daily Sport*.

When I subsequently lost my job on the *Sunday Mirror*, my wife Pauline broke the news to Steve, who was quick to telephone me with his sympathy and to give me shifts on the *Sport*. An act of kindness for which I shall forever be grateful.

Years later, when the aforementioned Des Kelly was driving Steve to an early grave, I only wish I could have been in a position to offer more than sympathy. Steve had joined the *Daily Mirror* as their main man in the north after leaving the *Sport* in 1992. It was his misfortune that Kelly, a man long on self-belief but short on talent, became sports editor (an example of bullshit, or blarney in his case, baffling brains). Kelly instructed his desk to put Steve under pressure, a despicable, prolonged process that involved the basic tactic of finding fault with just about everything Steve wrote and constantly demanding rewrites.

The effect of this upon Steve's health was never more apparent than in the immediate aftermath of Manchester United's dramatic, last-gasp Champions League Final victory against Bayern Munich in Barcelona in 1999. After the final whistle, the media were told that a UEFA official would escort them to the managers' press conference, which would be staged a long way from the press box situated high in one of the towering stands at the Camp Nou.

Neither Steve nor I could be accused of being slowcoaches when it came to hitting deadlines. Nevertheless, somehow we both missed the UEFA escort and found ourselves having to make our own way to the media room. The ensuing, seemingly endless trek through the labyrinthine corridors of the vast 90,000-seater stadium where everyone we asked for directions appeared clueless, was stressful enough for me. But so much worse for Steve, a man already under sustained pressure from Kelly and his acolytes.

We missed Sir Alex Ferguson's address to the media, relying upon colleagues to give us the quotes. But it's the sight of Steve, sweat pouring down his face in rivulets, that will forever be my clearest memory of that momentous night. At one point, as we stumbled along, I gave him my handkerchief, which I remember was soaked within seconds of him mopping his face.

A few months later I met Steve and Sylvia at yet another Open golf championship, and as Steve chatted to colleagues, I asked Sylvia how he was coping. 'Look at him Bill,' she said. 'I'm really worried for his health if he doesn't get out.'

The following week, after meeting Kelly in their London showdown, Steve made up his mind he was getting out of there and later agreed a severance package. His ordeal was over but I'm sure his sense of injustice must have been prolonged.

I suffered something similar to Steve's treatment, first at the *Sunday Mirror* and subsequently in my time at the *Daily Star*, although on neither occasion was the torment as protracted as it was for Steve.

He and Sylvia left the stress and strain of tabloid life behind for three years, swapping it for the stress and strain of running their pub, the Antelope, in Congleton, Cheshire.

Later he returned to the job that he was born to do, working for the *Daily Star Sunday*. I reckon he'd have gone on doing the job he loved well into his seventies had he been allowed to do so.

It was a privilege and a pleasure to work with and alongside Steve. And I'm delighted that we remain, and always will be, good friends.

PHIL THOMAS

(Daily Sport and *The Sun)*

IT WAS the greatest out-of-the-blue phone call I ever got
… although no boss has ever caused me more headaches
than Steve Millar. Nothing to do with bollockings or asking
the impossible, mind. Entirely down to the number of
vodkas I got through in our days together at the *Daily Sport*.

When Steve rang in early 1990, I was seriously worried
that I'd have to head back to London to find a job. And
having spent 18 months of the two years I'd worked there
previously trying to get back north, it wasn't an appealing
prospect.

But Phil Smith, Steve's number two, suggested my
name when he was looking for staff. He picked up the
phone and so began a friendship – it was more than a
working one from the off to be honest – as strong as any
I've made in journalism.

And talk about starting as you mean to go on. One day
before the off I broke my thumb, was told not to drive for
six weeks and had to make a very nervous call to my new
boss. It was hardly the greatest first impression.

'No problem,' said Steve, who only lived a couple of miles away from me in Warrington. 'I'll pick you up in the morning.' So, for the best part of my first two months on the *Daily Sport*, he ferried me to and from the office. Sports editor and chauffeur rolled into one.

But the best part was, at the time we only had one edition a week. So every day after a few hours' work we'd head for the Crown and Kettle next to the office, where trebles were a quid in happy hour. However, because Phil knew the landlord – he knew everyone really – it was happy hour all day for us. So I'd spend a fiver and get home slaughtered every night with door-to-door service from the boss. It was a damned shame when the doc said I could drive again, although I'm not sure my liver would say the same.

And while we all knew Steve was in charge, it was never really a boss-staff relationship. Not like any other I've ever had. Yep, he was the one making the decisions but there was no real sense of hierarchy. Not like most – make that all – the rest I've worked for.

I've been on papers for more than 35 years, nationals for three decades, and none has ever come close to those days on the *Daily Sport*. People may scoff at it but that remains far and away the most talented collection of journalists on any sports desk. But more than that. It was a gang of mates having a laugh. There was never a 'Monday morning' feeling about the start of the week. Sure, the work would get done, but it never felt like work. It was a laugh – and that stemmed from Steve first and foremost.

And if there was the slightest excuse for a party or a piss-up, you could be certain he wouldn't let it pass.

Night at Belle Vue dogs? Yep, on it straight away. A particularly raucous one, that ... Lindsay Sutton ended up being pelted in Scotch eggs before we'd even got in the building.

Rugby League Writers' Dinner? The *Daily Sport* was the first paper to book a table – and it had to be travel by minibus so everyone would be drinking. Especially Bob Jackson, the Aussie forward, who came as one of four Warrington players, and for some reason got it into his head it was a black tie do. It wasn't. At least he looked the part as he got so pissed that he challenged Widnes coach Doug Laughton to a head-butting contest. Then he fell off the bus going home and threw up all over his tux. The point being, Steve was egging him on as much as the rest of us.

And every year when it came to the Challenge Cup Final – I was covering rugby league at the time – we'd all head south. Steve and wife Sylvia, me and Kathy (I was still on wife number one back then), Phil Smith and Penny, Ken and Janet Hunt. A mass exodus and just a brilliant weekend with a match in the middle of it.

I've worked for plenty of bosses who couldn't tell you the name of their staff's other halves, but not Steve. He knew them all. He knew the kids' names. He knew the families as mates ... because they were, even though colleague Neil Batley went close to getting a smack in the mouth off Sylvia when it was Steve's hush-hush 40th birthday. Everyone was sworn to secrecy. No one breathed a word and Steve arrived at the do thinking he was just heading for a few Saturday night scoops. As he walked up to the entrance,

Neil was outside having a fag. When Steve asked what he was doing there, he didn't exactly think on his feet by replying, 'I'm here for your do.' Fill in the expletives from Sylvia yourselves.

And speaking of Steve knowing about the families, when my daughter Hannah was still a baby, I got a frantic call from Kathy one day saying she'd taken her to hospital. It wasn't a life-or-death issue but it was enough to send a new dad into a blind panic. Especially because I was between cars and travelling on the train.

I knew rushing out of work wouldn't be a problem but that wasn't enough for Steve. He immediately commandeered the guy who did all the driving for the *Daily Sport*, told him to drop everything else and get me to the hospital pronto. That one stuck in the memory more than all the laughs to be honest.

That's why Steve and Sylvia were one of the first couples on the guest list for each of my three weddings, although he let me down badly on the last one by ducking it. I'm still not convinced that a long-planned, already booked holiday in America was a good enough excuse.

In the later years, our professional paths crossed largely from sharing a car to the same press conferences or matches. Although the fun was now being sucked out of the industry to be replaced by a set of intense, chin-stroking take-themselves-too-seriously types, the trips to and from the training ground or stadium were filled with as many laughs as ever.

And there will always be those nights when we get together all these years later at the Red Lion in Stockton

Heath, Warrington, for a few pints and a giggle. The days when he was my boss may have long since passed, but he's still knocking hell out of my liver.

TONY 'STENGUN' STENSON

(Daily Mirror and *Daily Star Sunday)*

I FIRST came across Steve Millar when I thought the *Daily Mirror* sports editor Dave Balmforth was having an affair. I'd always arrive early at our office on the 21st floor of Canary Wharf in London Docklands and hear him whispering down the phone. Sometimes giggling like a love-struck teenager. I knew the boss was married and was intrigued. After several weeks of the same, I eventually asked our secretary who was he regularly speaking with each morning.

'It's Steve Millar, a Manchester freelance. They talk every day,' she replied.

With a few exceptions our sports editor hated the staff he inherited. He thought they were overpaid and useless, despite those *Mirror* journalists winning awards and regularly delivering daily exclusives. Balmforth managed to find a way to rid himself of three great guys during his dreadful reign. He loved hungry freelancers and to say he wasn't a nice bloke is an understatement.

I thought anyone who liked him must be one of the same cloth. But Steve first came into my eye-sight at a *Mirror* sports Christmas party. We eventually met and … well, he was a great bloke for a northerner.

Our friendship continued mainly by phone and Steve eventually joined the *Mirror* as their northern sports writer, only to be later shafted by an equally odious sports editor in Des Kelly a few years later.

I left the *Mirror* after almost 30 years. Well, I didn't actually leave, I was forced out in 2003. Then a year later the phone rang. It was Ray Ansbro, then the new sports editor of the *Daily Star Sunday*. He wanted help with their London edition after launching the new newspaper and mentioned that Steve had recommended me. I swiftly accepted the offer and Steve and I were back in harness. The fun times began. We worked hard but always under the mantra of 'work first, play later'.

Together we covered FA Cup finals, England internationals, Wimbledon tennis, but most of all golf. The Open and Ryder Cup were our speciality. Long hours but also fun times. It was a joy working with him. We grafted but also had time to look up and smell the roses.

Our media desk at every Open was a fun desk. So much so that other journalists would always gather around it to join in with the mickey-taking.

The *Daily Star Sunday* was new to the Open and Ryder Cup scene and wasn't accepted as a golfing paper, despite us giving more coverage than any other paper. Usually we provided eight pages every Sunday during the Open. We were often given desks that were so far at the back of the media centre that they were almost in the rough. We complained about needing seats nearer to the action and the R&A responded the following year ... putting us near the Swedes. They claimed they misheard our request.

Steve, no doubt, has gone through several of our escapades, both on and off duty. But one moment sums him up to me as both person and journalist. It was during an Open at Royal Liverpool when we both stepped out of the press tent to witness the action and try to gather stories. We walked across one fairway and Steve spotted a face he knew and called out. The man froze, cringed, almost afraid to turn. He eventually did and his face, once wry and taut, eventually broke into a huge smile. Neil Lennon, then managing Celtic first time around, recognised Steve. His anxiety was washed away. Managing Celtic is a tough call in a city where half love you and the other half don't. And I mean don't.

Lennon immediately relaxed and the pair rambled on like old pals. Steve had reported on Lennon when he played briefly for Manchester City during a time when hacks and players trusted each other. They would have a further professional relationship later when Lennon became boss of Bolton Wanderers.

Lennon clearly trusted Steve, as did most of the old City team, with Peter Barnes, Gary Owen and Asa Hartford regular after-match drinkers with Steve in Didsbury on the outskirts of Manchester. Mike Summerbee and Dennis Tueart before then were pals of Steve away from the game.

That moment with Neil Lennon said a lot about the Millarman as we call him. A good bloke on and off duty. My pal.

PAUL HETHERINGTON

(News of the World and *Daily Star Sunday)*

FRIDAY MORNINGS in the football season in the days when Sir Alex Ferguson was managing Manchester United meant an early start to the club's training ground at Carrington. Fergie on a Friday wasn't to be missed and his round of press conferences with every section of the media always ended with his session with the Sunday papers.

Early in 2003, I arrived for what proved to be a particularly significant presser – for me, the *Daily Star Sunday* and Steve Millar. Peter Fitton, after a brilliant career on *The Sun*, had joined the Sunday ranks by being recruited by the *Mail on Sunday* and he greeted me that day by saying, 'Hi pal, have you got a minute? There's something I need to discuss with you about a mutual friend – Steve Millar.'

The *Daily Star Sunday* had been launched in September 2002 with my role being football editor. We had three soccer writers at the time – me, Harry Pratt covering London and Vince Ellis in the Midlands. Peter wanted to know whether we were still recruiting and, if so, would I be interested in hiring Steve.

You bet I was. After swapping one side of the bar for the other when he became a pub landlord, Steve was looking for a return to journalism. This immediately appealed to me for a number of reasons. I knew Steve well but there was a lot more to it than that. I knew he'd bring experience and versatile ability to the paper as he could work inside or outside the office through operating as a sub-editor, in a potential news editor role on sport or being on the road as a reporter.

It was the latter that appealed to me as I needed help. At the time I was covering the north-west football patch – the capital of football – writing my own column, ghosting Manchester United legend Bryan Robson's column and reporting the big match on a Saturday wherever in the country it was being played.

I was also covering England, had the major responsibility for producing an exclusive back-page lead story and my Fridays were manic. They usually involved travelling to three press conferences to see Fergie at United, Kevin Keegan at Manchester City and Gerard Houllier at Liverpool. I was getting home at 6pm and then had to start writing up three press conferences. It wasn't working for me or the sports editor Ray Ansbro, who was having to wait for my copy.

So it was no surprise when Ray agreed with me that appointing Steve would benefit the production of the paper. It would free me up on a Friday to cover one press conference and then concentrate on bashing the phone to get stories while Steve mopped up the other pressers on the patch.

I'd known Steve since I moved to Manchester from the north-east to join the *News of the World* in 1988. He was on the *Sunday Mirror* and was later sports editor of the *Daily Sport* and we met up from time to time for a pint or plenty. I knew we'd work well together and that's the way it panned out for the next 15 years. We'd cover big matches at home and abroad, with me reporting the match and Steve, a fine wordsmith, writing an overview of the major occasion. Or as it was known in the game, a colour piece.

Our travels took us to World Cups in Germany and South Africa, England matches in Israel, Qatar and Ukraine, Champions League finals in Europe and regularly to Wembley for big occasions such as FA Cup finals and England matches.

We had some fun and laughs, although I'm not sure Steve appreciated the call I made to him from Sun City in South Africa when he was back in England and attempting to check in for his flight to Johannesburg. Using my worst South African accent, I pretended to be from the tourist board there and bombarded him with questions about his forthcoming trip, which tours he'd like to go on and which animals he wanted to see. Flustered and preoccupied as he checked in for his flight to South Africa, he remained polite – but I knew what he wanted to say in response. That was even more the case when he realised it was a hoax and I was behind it.

And there were some highly-charged, pressure situations in some of those big-event trips. Ones that particularly come to mind are the Bayern Munich-Chelsea Champions League Final in 2012 and the England-Portugal World

Cup quarter-final in Germany in Gelsenkirchen six years earlier. Both those matches went to penalties in the most dramatic circumstances late on Saturday nights, which pushed to the limit the job of filing your copy on time to beat the deadline.

I recall Steve, like me, ad-libbing on a phone directly to the copy taker in England, having to leave his seat in the press box because he couldn't hear himself speak. But he managed, of course, to file his copy on time from another part of the stadium.

To add to the drama that night, England went out of the World Cup after a winking Cristiano Ronaldo was accused of getting Wayne Rooney – his Manchester United team-mate – sent off.

Talk about a busy night, because once the penalty shoot-out ended, there was only the briefest of windows for the pair of us to grab quotes from managers and players and file their reaction to the sensational events of that night.

And after Chelsea won the Champions League on penalties in Munich, the match finished so late that all public transport had ended for the night and Steve and I, plus other colleagues, found ourselves stranded at the out-of-town Allianz Arena. We ended up attempting to thumb a lift from the side of the autobahn before managing to flag down a taxi to take us to our hotel in Munich.

Inevitably, we headed straight to the bar to celebrate what we considered to be a job well done. With us, it was always a case of work hard, play hard. And I like to think we did both rather well.

JOHN RICHARDSON

(Daily Mail, The Sun and *Sunday Express)*

IT WAS a partnership that often had people chuckling. Laurel and Hardy. Hinge and Bracket. Statler and Waldorf. But did it produce results? Of course it did. Millar and Richardson was an enjoyable journalistic pairing that provided hours of great fun and acres of revealing copy. It certainly enriched my working life and I hope it was the same for Steve.

The double act became so renowned over the years that whenever we went solo it was often a case of 'how's your mate?'

Through the natural chemistry we were able to relax our interviewees and coax out of them exclusive tales. There was no softness. We knew what we wanted and in reporter parlance the grenade did go down the trousers but only when we thought the time was right to ask the crucial question.

I'd known Steve from an early age and always admired his work but I believe where we really clicked for the first time was on a Newcastle United tour to the Far East. Alan Shearer had just signed for the Toon in a £15m world record transfer and Newcastle announced that he'd be joining the club on their pre-season trip.

The fact that he never got to play a single minute was beside the point as, between us, Steve and I managed to manufacture a back-page lead pretty well every day. Also with us was Colin Young, who had just joined *The Sun* after my departure for the *Daily Mail,* and the *Newcastle Chronicle*'s Alan Oliver.

The trip featured a friendly in Osaka, Japan. Really, with Shearer unable to play because of red tape, the match was of little consequence. We were ushered into a private box where Jeremy Walker, who used to work in the north-east but who was now employed in Japan, joined us. He came up the steps that led into the private box sweating like mad in the humidity. 'You obviously haven't acclimatised yet Jez,' we laughed.

Well, after a few minutes Jeremy pointed to the adjoining private box and informed us that Arsène Wenger – then manager of Japanese side Grampus Eight – was in situ. He knew Arsène quite well and offered to introduce us. 'Yes,' I replied. 'That would be great.' Steve was nonplussed. He wasn't bothered.

Anyway, Arsène duly entered our box and I was introduced to him. I asked whether he minded conducting a quick interview on football in Japan. Steve remained seated, disinterested but within earshot. I asked Arsène about Glenn Hoddle, who was the England manager, with the pair having been together at Monaco.

'Oh,' replied Arsène, 'he has asked me to become the FA's technical director.'

Well, you've never seen Steve move so quickly. He was out of his seat like a shot and shaking a startled Arsène's hand. 'I'm Steve Millar of the *Daily Mirror*,' he said, turning on his Dictaphone. He knew a back-page lead when he heard one – WENGER TO BE OFFERED ENGLAND JOB.

As it happened, Arsène turned it down and just a few months later was announced as Arsenal's new manager. 'Arsène Who?' screamed the headlines. Well we knew who he was now.

But it hasn't always been plain sailing with the mighty duo as a trip to Blackpool's rundown training ground proved. We'd both been to the 2010 World Cup finals in South Africa and were looking for a nice pre-season feature. Blackpool, under Ian Holloway, had just been promoted to the Premier League. We both knew Ian was a good talker so why not pop in at the training ground? We were certain he'd be pleased to see us.

On a nice summer's day we turned up and ventured towards one of the portacabins, having guessed where Ian and the players would be. Suddenly we were stopped in our tracks by an overweight character who appeared to be toothless except for one lone front molar.

'Who the hell are you and what are you doing here?' he yelled. After a quick explanation implying that we were doing Blackpool a favour, he was in unrelenting mood. 'You don't just pop in at Manchester United's training ground so you're not doing that here,' he barked. There was no reasoning. We were manhandled off the premises.

This was our first meeting with Matt Williams who was the Blackpool secretary and who out of adversity was to become a good friend and a useful contact. Glad to say he now enjoys a full complement of teeth.

Together with Steve, we've made many friends and contacts and one prominent football person once had Steve on 'drugs'. Mind you, they could never be performance-enhancing could they?

We'd gone to see the Wigan owner Dave Whelan who was always good for a feature or two. After the interview, Dave informed us that he was often wobbly on his feet at first after getting out of a chair.

'I've been given tablets to help,' Dave explained.

'Oh,' replied Steve. 'The same thing has started happening to me.' That was the cue for Dave to search out his own tablets and hand them over to Steve.

'There you go, try these,' he said.

Unbelievably, Steve took them and said, 'Many thanks Dave. I'll give them a go.'

Life with Sir Alex Ferguson (plain Alex for most of our careers) was never dull. Bans were handed out like confetti to the media. Relationships would sometimes be very strained, although that didn't prevent Steve and me being regularly slapped on the head as Fergie made his way to his press conference table.

During one period, the atmosphere had soured even among the Sunday papers, who generally enjoyed a better relationship with the boss of bosses. By now, Steve was on the *Daily Star Sunday*, although he preferred to tell people he worked for the *Sunday Express*. We'd had enough of the cold war and as two of the senior members decided to try to sort it out. So after another fractious session, we decided to race after Alex and head him off outside the doors of the training ground.

Steve opened up with a few words before being deafened by a fusillade of expletives from the great man. Once that was over, on Alex resuming a relationship, Steve said, 'I suppose that's a no then?' Cue another volley of abuse.

It was one of the few times we didn't end up with what we wanted. Mostly we came back with the goods. But nothing lasts forever, so when Steve reluctantly rode off into the sunset it was like Morecambe without Wise. Ant without Dec.

But no one can take away the memories. Thanks Steve for being a great reporting partner. But even better, a great mate.